MIRAGE IN THE MIRROR

FINDING YOUR BEST SELF

Rachael Montgomery Morua

Rachael Montgomery Morua

Dedication

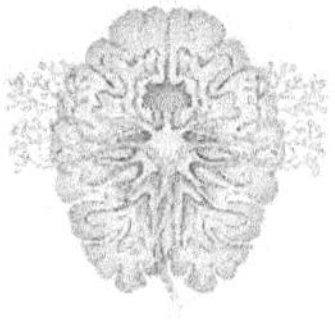

This book is dedicated to the clients, patients, and students who, over the years, trusted me with their vulnerability.

You allowed me into moments of uncertainty, pain, growth, and quiet courage. Thank you. Your willingness to speak what felt difficult, to stay present when it would have been easier to turn away, and to remain open in the face of discomfort has been a profound privilege to witness.

You shared your stories without knowing how they would unfold. You showed up honestly, even when clarity felt distant. In doing so, you taught me as much as I ever hoped to offer in return. This work carries your resilience, your questions, and your determination to keep moving forward.

I am grateful for the trust you placed in me and for the space you made for this work to exist. Being invited into your journey has been an honor I do not take lightly.

This book is written with you in mind, with respect for your courage, your humanity, and the depth it takes to be seen.

Acknowledgment

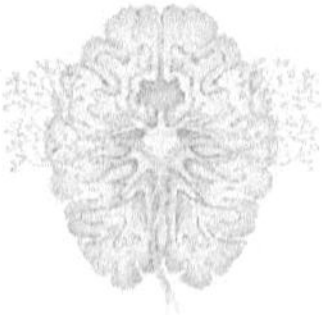

This book exists because of many quiet contributions, offered in ways that will never be fully visible on the page.

Thank you to all my mentors, supervisors, and colleagues, both past and current, for the guidance, challenges, and discipline you brought into my work life. Each conversation, consultation, and moment of thoughtful disagreement sharpened my thinking and deepened my respect for this work. I am especially grateful to those who modeled integrity not just in technique, but in how they showed up as people. I hold my brother, Dr. Aaron Montgomery, in particular regard, as he has always been my role model, closest confidant, and a trusted colleague with whom I exchange ideas. I also honor my mother, Vita Montgomery, who taught me to question everything, nurtured intellectual curiosity, and consistently offered unwavering support.

To the clinicians who continue to question, refine, and elevate the field, thank you for holding complexity without rushing toward certainty. Your commitment to ethical practice, curiosity, and continued learning makes this work possible and sustainable.

To my family, my husband Mariano, and close friends—particularly Leviticus Jelks—thank you for your patience and quiet support. Writing this book required time, focus, and emotional presence that often extended beyond the page. Your steadiness made that possible. Thank you for offering grounding, perspective, and humor when it was needed most.

Finally, to the reader, thank you for engaging with this book honestly. Not for agreeing with every idea, but for being willing to pause, reflect, and examine yourself without distortion. That willingness is rare, and it matters.

This book was written with deep respect for the complexity of being human.

If it has helped you see yourself with greater clarity, responsibility, or compassion, then it has done what it was meant to do.

Disclaimer

The case studies and clinical examples presented in this book are entirely fictional. While they are informed by the author's professional experience as a licensed therapist and are intended to reflect common psychological patterns and therapeutic challenges, they do not represent any specific individual, past or present.

Any resemblance to actual persons, living or dead, or to real-life events or locales is purely coincidental. These examples have been created solely for illustrative and educational purposes to demonstrate the concepts and techniques discussed in this book.

Medical Disclaimer

The information provided in this book is for educational purposes only and is not intended as a substitute for professional medical or mental health advice, diagnosis, or treatment. Always seek the advice of your physician or another qualified mental health provider with any questions you may have regarding a medical or psychological condition.

Reading this book does not establish a therapist–patient relationship between the reader and the author.

About the Author

Rachael Montgomery Morua is a Licensed Marriage and Family Therapist, Certified Sex Therapist, and PhD Candidate for Clinical Sexology as well as an Adjunct Professor whose work centers on the intersection of emotional regulation, relational integrity, and embodied self-awareness. Her clinical approach is grounded in a simple premise: lasting change does not come from insight alone, but from the capacity to act with coherence under emotional pressure.

With advanced training in psychotherapy, hypnotherapy, clinical sexology, and neuro-psychotherapy, Rachael integrates evidence-based and somatic modalities, including EMDR, biofeedback, and yoga psychology, to help individuals and couples move beyond intellectual understanding into lived integration. Her work focuses on how the nervous system, attachment patterns, and relational dynamics interact to shape behavior, intimacy, and resilience.

As a Certified Sex Therapist, Rachael specializes in intimacy, communication, human sexuality, and sexual well-being, areas often surrounded by silence, shame, or avoidance. She is known for creating a clinical space that is direct, grounded, and free of judgment, where difficult conversations can be approached with clarity rather than urgency.

In addition to her therapeutic practice, Rachael is an EMDR Certified Therapist, a Clinical Supervisor, and a mentor to developing clinicians. Her work with complex trauma, PTSD, anxiety, depression, and relational distress is informed by a neurobiological understanding of stress and recovery, as well as a deep respect for the discipline required to sustain change over time.

What distinguishes Rachael's work is her emphasis on responsibility without harshness and compassion without avoidance. She challenges the notion that healing is a passive or purely emotional process, instead guiding clients toward self-governance, congruence, and durable change.

Mirage in the Mirror reflects the same principles that guide her clinical work: clarity over reassurance, integration over insight, and accountability as a form of self-respect.

Preface

Before change can take shape, you need clarity on why you opened this book. The first moment of honesty, recognizing that something in you needs attention, direction, or refinement, is the real starting point of this process.

What prompts you to embark on this transformative journey through these pages? Is it your desire to change? Do you long for personal growth? Or perhaps it is the curiosity of what lies beyond your current boundaries? Whatever your reason may be, acknowledging that something within you feels unsettled is the first step toward understanding what moves you and beginning the change you seek.

This is where intention becomes your ally. Research consistently shows that having clear objectives increases the chances of success in personal development endeavors. Therefore, it is crucial to contemplate what you are trying to achieve through this. Take a moment to articulate your aspirations, whether they revolve around gaining self-confidence, overcoming obstacles, or cultivating healthier habits, so that you can lay the groundwork for tangible outcomes you desire.

Now, as you have come this far, let me share a secret with you. Defining these objectives empowers you to stay focused and motivated along the way. It fosters resilience and determination to face and overcome the challenges that may slow your pace on the road to progress.

Think of this journey as a thrilling adventure of self-discovery. So, get excited about discovering new things about yourself and finding abilities you didn't know you had.

Chinese philosopher Lao Tzu once said, "The journey of a thousand miles begins with a single step." This means that no matter how BIG your goal is, you can achieve it if you simply take the very first step.

And you have already taken that step. So, with enthusiasm and purpose, let us dive into the pages ahead and search for what you came looking for.

Now, let's get started on getting to know yourself!

Contents

Chapter 1: Start Your Day with Mindfulness

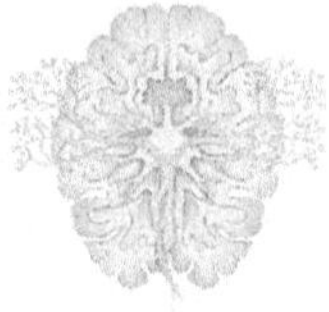

"What day is it?" asked Pooh.

"It's today," squeaked Piglet.

"My favorite day," said Pooh.

The inseparable duo, Pooh and Piglet, may live only in stories, but their story reminds us to take pleasure in every moment and consider every day as if it were the best we had. Of course, easier said than done, right? This is where mindfulness comes into the picture. And before we learn to apply this practice in our daily lives, let's see what it actually means.

Thanks to the internet, 'mindfulness' has become more of a buzzword than serving its intended purpose. That purpose is simple, yet challenging: it's the practice of quieting your ever-wandering train of thought. Mindfulness isn't about doing more but about being fully present. If you dissect the word, you find "mind" and "fullness," a reminder to engage your awareness completely in the here and now. In our pursuit of dreams and excellence, it's easy to become entangled in the hustle of daily life. Studies have shown that an average millennial has more workplace burnout than previous generations. With increasing workload and intensifying competition within the job market, people are prompted to lose the sense of meaningfulness in their lives. Amidst these busy routines, we are led astray from life's important details. But what detail is more important than ourselves?

Most people spend a major chunk of their daily lives on autopilot. Autopilot is a mental state where routine tasks are delegated to the mechanical parts of your brain. In neurobiology, your brain receives signals in the form of electrical impulses called synapses. When generated, these impulses create a pattern of activating our brain cells, called neurons. The more we practice an act, the more deeply ingrained these synaptic impulses become, making us prone to complete a task without any external help. This mechanism is how we master skills and perform several of our everyday activities without any hassle.

However, its major drawback does not go unnoticed. While your body runs on autopilot, your mind is free to wander, and it often travels to the past or future, leaving the present moment unattended.

Our brains are wired for efficiency, conserving energy by default. This is why complex tasks like quadratic equations or deep conversations can feel daunting; they demand focused, effortful thinking. This energy-saving instinct can lead us into unproductive cycles, worrying about the future or replaying regrets from the past. One of my clients, Mrs. K., described her mornings this way: "I realized I'd driven to work completely on autopilot. I couldn't even remember a single stoplight. I'd eaten breakfast, but I didn't remember and couldn't tell you what it tasted like. I always felt like I was physically present but mentally somewhere else entirely. Oftentimes, I'd be replaying yesterday's argument or rehearsing tomorrow's presentation." This is the autopilot state many of us live in daily...

Leaving our bodies to this autopilot machinery, we let our minds wander away. So, when you sit down on the chair and grab the fork and knife to slice your chicken, your autopilot remains in control, while your mind stays occupied with the text you received from your ex last week. When you enter the bathroom to take a shower, your autopilot takes charge of the entire process, and your mind remains engaged with the meeting at the workplace and the pending assignments, or if you had earned more, you would be much better off. Mindfulness is the antidote to autopilot. Before we go further, try this simple exercise. In the space provided, list what distracts you most throughout your day. It could be a type of activity, a specific person, a project, or a place. Write down whatever comes to mind.

I am distracted by:

____

____

____

____

Identifying your main distractions is a powerful first step toward mindfulness. It helps you regain control by interrupting the repetitive thought loops you've grown accustomed to.

To deepen your understanding, try one more exercise. In the table below, write down as many details of your experiences as you can. If you need more space, use a notebook or the pages at the end of the chapter.

	Write down your mindfulness experiences below. (Try to express In as much detail as possible)
Where are you while reading this book?	
How does it feel in your hands?	
What does the texture of this book feel like?	

Describe what this book looks like to you.	
Can you smell it? If yes, what does it smell like?	
Are you eating or drinking something as well? If so, write down your experience.	
What noises do you hear right now?	
Do you have other things on your mind right now that are distracting you?	
Scan your body; what is your body feeling right now, and where?	

Mindfulness is about awakening to the vivid details of the beautiful world around you. From the grand scale of the universe down to nature's minute patterns, there is endless depth to notice, yet we often rush past it, forgetting how precious and fleeting our chance to truly see can be.

Therefore, beginning your day with mindfulness allows you to experience its deepest benefits right from the start.

A New Routine for a New You

The path toward a mindful day begins the moment you wake up. As you get ready to start your day ahead, try giving your morning routine more time and space. For example, instead of waking up at 8 in the morning when you have to reach work at 9, try waking up a little earlier. You can set your intention by taking deep breaths as you get up in bed. This simple act helps center your nervous system and energizes you for the day ahead.

Read through the exercise below before your next shower, and bring this awareness into the experience. As you stand under the shower, pay close attention to the water hitting your skin—the way it bounces or slides away. Notice the temperature of the water. Is it warm? Is it cold? How does the temperature of the water feel on your entire body? Let that sensation relax your muscles and awaken your senses as the warmth or cold seeps into your skin.

Now, engage your other senses. As you stand under the shower, notice the fragrances rising with the steam. Where do these scents come from? Which notes can you identify in your soap or shower gel? Observe the water splashing down and forming tiny streams along your torso, thighs, and calves. Look at the droplets on the walls, and notice how they catch and reflect the light, if any. Watch how the droplets chase one another as they merge together and fall with gravity. Listen to the whooshing of the water and the gentle splashes against your skin. Tune into the softer sounds in the background, any echoes, drips, or movements in the room. Let each sound anchor you more fully in the moment.

If you'd like, let a small splash of water touch your lips, noticing its freshness. Feel the stream on your skin, allowing yourself to be present in the moment. And as you extend your hand to touch the knob to turn it off, notice the texture and temperature of the material against your fingers. Acknowledge your simple control over this small part of your environment. Finally, as you step out and dry off, feel how the towel's fibers absorb each bead of water from your skin. Now that you have completed this mindful start to your day, write about your entire experience below.

Write down what you noticed in the shower.

____

____

____

____

____

____

The Power of Being Alone

Seeing someone talk to themselves might seem unusual, and many people are quick to attach negative labels. Yet the truth is, self-talk is common and often healthy. Among people who talk to themselves, introverts are the most susceptible to this habit. However, extroverts with extended social circles have also been found to have indulged in pep talks with themselves.

Some studies suggest that the type of self-talk matters more than the personality of the person using it. For example, researchers at the University of Michigan found that using positive, encouraging, or distant self-talk can boost confidence and emotional regulation.[1]

In another study conducted in the United Kingdom, children who had a habit of talking to themselves achieved higher grades and were more emotionally intelligent than those who didn't.[2] Emotional intelligence itself is often misunderstood, but its value is clear: it is fundamental for building meaningful relationships and achieving personal goals.

---

[1] Gainsburg, I., & Kross, E. (2020). Distanced self-talk changes how people conceptualize the self. Journal of Experimental Social Psychology, 88, 103969. https://doi.org/10.1016/j.jesp.2020.103969

[2] "I Will Do My Very Best!" Children Who Engage in Positive Self-Talk About Effort Can Boost Their Math Achievement | Society for Research in Child Development SRCD. (2019, December 17). Srcd.org. https://www.srcd.org/news/i-will-do-my-very-best-children-who-engage-positive-self-talk-about-effort-can-boost-their

"Talking to oneself, I have often thought, is the best way to be sure of intelligent and witty conversation."

-Grant Morrison.

With this in mind, try this: stand in front of a mirror and have a gentle conversation with yourself. Speak out loud, with clarity. Offer yourself appreciation and express gratitude. Notice your reflection, your body, alive and present, and stay with this awareness for a few minutes. If it helps, imagine you're speaking to your most trusted confidant. When you're ready, set an intention by briefly stating your agenda for the day. Then, in the space below, write at least five positive affirmations that reflect who you are, who you are becoming, or what you wish to continue nurturing.

I am ____

I am ____

I am ____

I am ____

I am ____

You have come so far, and I am so proud of you!

Let's move ahead. This is often the moment for a rushed breakfast, eaten while scrolling through a phone. But now, since you're practicing mindfulness, I'm afraid you'll have to bid farewell to those old rituals.

A mindful breakfast is one where you gather your full attention and offer it entirely to the food in front of you. Take your time with your meal. Set aside all distractions as you prepare your coffee, tea, protein drink, or whatever morning beverage you enjoy. Savor the aroma rising from your cup and notice how it swirls in your mouth as you take a sip. Pay attention to the flavors in your mouth as you take each bite. Sit back and pay close attention to the textures and subtle details of your meal.

When I first introduced Mr. S., a software engineer, to the concept of mindful eating, he was skeptical. "I've been eating breakfast for forty-two years," he said flatly. "I think I know how to eat." But he agreed to try the exercise anyway.

The following week, he returned to our session visibly changed. "I need to tell you something strange," he began. "I've been drinking the same brand of coffee every single morning for probably fifteen years.

This week, when I actually paid attention, I discovered I don't even like this coffee. It's too bitter. I've been drinking something I don't enjoy for fifteen years and never noticed. And that made me wonder: what else in my life am I doing on autopilot? What else have I never actually questioned or truly experienced? It was just coffee, but it felt like waking up from a very long sleep."

When we bring mindful attention to even the simplest acts, we often discover we've been sleepwalking through experiences we assumed we knew well.

Write down what you had for breakfast and what you noticed about it.

____

____

____

____

____

____

____

To build on this, consider your journey to your first destination of the day. Try not to rush, even if it means waking up a little earlier. You can try walking if the place isn't too far away, or you might choose to park your vehicle a bit farther than usual to walk those extra steps. And as you walk by, try staying present within your surroundings—take in the sights, sounds, smells, and the feel of the world around you. In a world filled with screens and constant distractions, it's natural for the mind to wander. As long as it is fine to let your mind wander, your primary intention should be to gently guide your attention back to the present moment. If it's the meeting with your boss, friend, or a family member you're fretting about as you sit down to have your morning beverages, simply acknowledge the thought, then return your focus to the warmth and weight of the cup in your hand. Now, pause for a moment of reflection. In the space below, write down what you noticed about your morning routine today.

If you could change your morning routine, how would it be?

____

____

____

____

____

Follow the practice of mindfulness you have learned throughout this chapter. Of course, this cannot be achieved overnight, and neither do I expect you to do so. However, your determination for a mindful life should not be shaken by fleeting thoughts or automatic actions.

"Each morning, we are born again. What we do today is what matters most."

– Buddha

"Thoughts and feelings are like mud in a glass of stirred water. Mindfulness practice allows the mud to settle to the bottom of the glass, making the water clear."

-Thích Nhất Hạnh

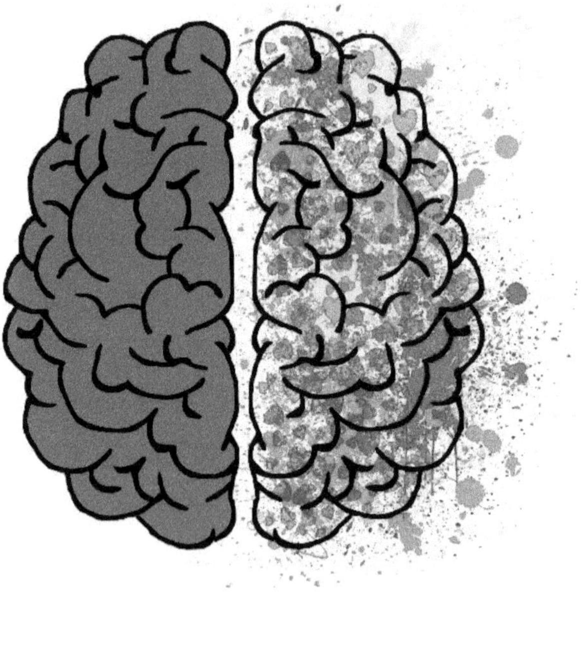

Notes for Chapter 1

Key Takeaways

- **Mindfulness is all about staying aware of your surroundings and the present moment.**
- **The purpose of mindfulness is to drag you away from the worries of your past and the pessimistic prospects of your future.**
- **Mindfulness can be achieved by simplistic techniques applied and practiced within our daily routines.**
- **The pursuit of mindfulness begins as you start your day in the morning.**
- **Starting mindfully and by staying aware of your surroundings, which includes giving attention to the most trivial parts of your everyday life.**
- **Self-talk can alter your perceptions positively and affect your self-esteem.**
- **Self-talk can improve your emotional intelligence.**
- **Make use of your five senses as you go about your pursuit of a mindful experience.**

Chapter 2: Hi Self! It's Nice to Meet You!

All right, let me ask you a quick question before we begin. How many hours do you spend scrolling through your social media feeds, observing someone else's life each day? Of course, the answer will vary depending on your lifestyle, schedule, aspirations, and everything else we consider important.

If you're thinking I'm about to launch into a series of judgments against people who love social media, rest assured, that will not be the case at all. People are making a living off of social media and are using these platforms to spread positivity around the world as well. But this book isn't about judging others; it's about how judgment harms the judge.

When we judge others, we usually end up thinking about our own faults, too. This makes us worry that others might be judging us as well. Choosing to withhold judgment helps quiet that internal critic.

Holding onto judgment comes at a high personal cost. It creates internal stress, which can weaken your immune system and harm your health. Being judgmental pushes people away, hindering meaningful connections and increasing loneliness, which is linked to serious health risks. Often, a judgmental stance is less about others and more about our own unaddressed insecurities, which stifles genuine growth. Positive energy attracts others, while negativity repels. The core truth is that releasing judgment is fundamental for building healthier relationships and personal well-being.

If you're thinking, *"Alright, but what* is *judgment?"* take a breath. Trust that we're getting there. If this is what you are wondering at the moment, I need you to take a deep breath and give your trust to this book—the work of my heart—where every part serves your journey.

In the first chapter, we explored mindfulness, the practice of anchoring yourself in the present moment. In this chapter, you will meet the most important person in your life: the one who deserves your attention, beyond all the faces on your screens. I suspect you know who I mean. If not, stand up and look in the mirror. The person you see is the one we're here to meet, the constant companion who has weathered every storm with you. The one we are to meet. But how do we know if it really is the most important person in your life? Well, let's form a list of what this person has done for you:

- **Supporting you in every single one of your struggles and hardships in life**

- **Wiping the warm-turning-cold tears at the end of every misery**
- **Staying by your side, whether during stomach-hurting laughter or gut-wrenching anxieties**
- **Always has your back!**
- **Has helped you make important life decisions**
- **Has been there to celebrate every one of your successes**
- **Feeds you, dresses you, bathes you**

Now, imagine your reflection was a separate person who could hear and understand you. What would you say?

We would simply scream, growl, and scold ourselves for every stupid mistake. We might shriek in anger, "You idiot! What on earth made you do such a stupid thing?"—watching our reflection flinch under the barrage like a child caught red-handed. There's a dark appeal in that, a release for our inner critic.

Or you can choose a different path. Praise your reflection on the achievements you have made, no matter how small. Pat yourself on the back and say, "What an amazing job I've done!" Smile, wink, and applaud. Appreciate yourself and feel content with your accomplishments.

This act of self-introduction is vital. It strengthens confidence that might otherwise falter at minor setbacks. If life is like a party where your role is to keep dancing, small setbacks are like tiny blisters that can slow you down. They're painful and can sideline you temporarily, but they're also part of the process. They force a recovery period—a necessary pause so you can return to the dance floor stronger and more capable than before, leaving the audience enthralled and mesmerized. They are awed and thrilled because no one had anticipated such a performance from you, not even yourself. But would you have achieved this if you hadn't taken the time to know yourself and accept each inconvenience as a mere recovery period?

Let's try a simple exercise. Use the following spaces to write down all those things that you think you could have done better in life.

I could have____

I could have____

I could have____

I could have____

I could have____

The list above carries some, if not all, of your regrets and condemnations. I invite you to see it from another angle. What if the things you've been blaming yourself for are actually the very things that held you back? What if that constant self-criticism has stolen the faith you needed to move forward? If there is one thing I could tell you about regrets, it is that they've never brought someone peace, let alone a contented life. However, growing out of painful experiences isn't a cakewalk, but it becomes possible once you stop fighting yourself and start listening.

This is why knowing yourself matters. It's how you learn to navigate life's challenges with clarity and emerge stronger from them. In my practice, I frequently hear from people who feel they are being chased by their own thoughts. One individual, let's call him Mr. D, shared an account that perfectly describes this state of chronic mental overactivity and emotional exhaustion:

"It's constant. My girlfriend sometimes gets upset with me because if I'm not talking to her, I'll pull out my phone and start reading social media. I do it to focus on literally anything other than my own mind. Hyper-anxiety is my guess. I've never been officially diagnosed, but my mind constantly races.

I don't think the issue is being alone. It's a natural human instinct to avoid pain, and even then, no one said anything about having painful thoughts. I can't speak for everyone, but for me, what gets exhausting is how my mind is always in overdrive. It isn't that I'm thinking cruel or sad thoughts (mostly); it's that no matter what I do, say, or take to relax, my thoughts continually flood me. It's like my mind is Chrome with 50 tabs open, switching between each one, and as a result, I function sluggishly."

When Mr. D describes his mind as having '50 tabs open,' he is giving us a perfect window into Sympathetic Activation. In this state, the body is flooded with the "get up and go" energy meant for survival, but because there is no physical "lion" to run from, that energy gets trapped in the mind. It manifests as racing thoughts, a need for constant distraction, and a feeling of being 'wired but tired.' As a therapist, I see Mr. D's struggle as the body's attempt to stay 'ready' for a threat that never arrives. This chronic state of high alert eventually drains the battery, which, as we will see later with Mark, can eventually lead the body to flip the emergency breaker into a total shutdown.

To place Mr. D's experience in a broader human context, it can be helpful to pause and reflect on how we have understood struggle itself across time and wisdom traditions. The following quotations invite us to soften our judgment of inner chaos and consider the possibility that even relentless mental activity may be pointing toward growth rather than failure.

"There are no mistakes."

-Sigmund Freud

"There are no mistakes in life, only lessons. There is no such thing as a negative experience, only opportunities to grow, learn, and advance along the road of self-mastery. From struggle comes strength. Even pain can be a wonderful teacher."

-Robin Sharma

Rather than holding these words only as ideas, the next step is to let the body and nervous system have a direct experience of what they point toward. A visualization activity can help you move from insight into felt safety.

Now, let's Do A Guided Visualization

Take a moment with this guided visualization. Read it through once or twice, then close your eyes and follow it, or have someone read it aloud to you. Wherever you are at the moment, whether sitting down on a chair, half lying on a couch, or lying down on the floor or bed, try closing your eyes for a few moments. As you close your eyes, bring an image of yourself to mind, but as if you're meeting for the very first time. This is a stranger you're getting to know. Greet yourself and observe, ask questions, and perceive your own movements in the imaginary world. Bring the image to life by paying attention to the smallest details. You may begin by noticing your facial features or maybe your hair and clothes.

Watch as this version of you moves and speaks. How do you carry yourself? What questions would you ask someone you're genuinely curious about? Take your time here, make jokes; this is your chance to meet yourself free from past stories, just presence and curiosity.

When you're ready, open your eyes and write about the experience below, as if you were taking notes on someone fascinating you just met.

Write about this experience in the following space.

____

____

____

____

____

____

____

You might be feeling a lot right now. Let's explore those emotions, but first, let's look at the incredible organ making all of this possible: your brain and what it's actually doing.

INTERNAL STRUCTURE OF THE BRAIN

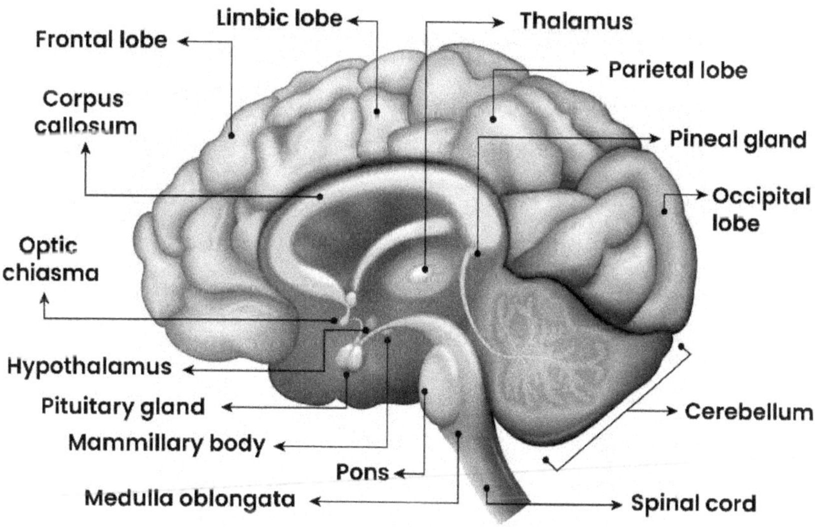

Figure 3.1 The Limbic System[3]

Let's talk about the brilliant, emotional computer in your head: your brain. Have you ever heard of your *hippocampus*? This is the part of the brain within the inner folds of the temporal lobe that stores long-term memories.

It works closely with the limbic system—the emotional control center—and a key structure called the *amygdala*. Think of the amygdala as your internal alarm bell. It triggers fear, anger, and stress responses. The hippocampus doesn't just store memories; it also helps regulate that alarm. When the amygdala sounds the alarm (activating your "fight or flight" response), the hippocampus steps in to help cool the system down. Together, these structures shape how you feel and react. But your emotional brain does more than just react; it's deeply connected to your body's entire operating system, including what we call the "fight or flight" response.

This is where your endocrine system comes in, acting as a key chemical messenger network rather than the body's primary command center. Hormones control and coordinate your body's metabolism, energy level, reproduction, growth and development, and responses to injury, stress, and mood. The system regulates how much of each hormone is released, which influences—rather than solely determines—our emotional states. This regulation affects how we feel and respond to different situations. While hormones provide the

---

[3] Designed by Magnific

chemical foundation for these shifts, they do not act in a vacuum; instead, they operate in constant dialogue with the body's neural pathways.

Porges (2011) developed the polyvagal theory, which focuses on the autonomic nervous system (ANS) and its role in regulating emotional and physiological responses.[4] It emphasizes the role of the vagus nerve in controlling the parasympathetic nervous system (PNS), which promotes calm and relaxation. To bridge these ideas, polyvagal theory explains the *neural* mechanisms that interact with and often direct the hormonal responses described above. The theory proposes that our physiological state is governed by three primary neural circuits:

1. The Ventral Vagal Complex (VVC): Associated with our social engagements and calm states.
2. The Sympathetic Nervous System (SNS): Related to our "fight or flight" responses.
3. The Dorsal Vagal Complex (DVC): Linked to our immobilization and shutdown responses.

While these terms help us map the biology of the brain, they can feel abstract until you hear what it actually feels like when the "shutdown" response takes over a person's life. I

[4] Porges, S. W. (2011). The polyvagal theory: Neurophysiological foundations of emotions, attachment, communication, and self-regulation. W W Norton & Co.

regularly see clients who feel they have simply "lost" themselves.

They aren't just tired or sad; they are experiencing what we call Dorsal Vagal Shutdown. This is the body's most extreme survival strategy, a biological "emergency brake." When the nervous system decides that the stress we are facing is too overwhelming to fight or flee, it simply clicks off to protect us. It's a physiological state of numbness and disconnection, essentially a "faint" response that leaves a person feeling like a ghost in their own life. To understand the weight of this biological retreat, we have to look past the clinical definition and listen to the internal experience of those living within it. One of my clients, a man I'll call Mr. M, once recounted his struggle with a clarity that captures the sheer isolation of this state:

"It's devastating how much of my life I've missed out on because I've felt completely numb and checked out for so long. I've been trapped in this state for three years. I don't even remember what it's like to have feelings and to be present in the world. I miss so many things about my old life. I am 32 years old and these should be the best years of my life, but they are absolute misery.

I don't know how I'll ever get out of this. Ignoring it, accepting it, focusing on life—none of it has helped. My system is in a complete shutdown. I'm so far down the 'freeze' response that I feel completely and utterly trapped. I had a good life before this with many things I loved and enjoyed, but now I have no access to my memories, to my sense of self, or to the world happening around me. I feel no weather, no seasons, no time.

I've had so much blood work done, tried many medications, and many therapists. I even worked through a year of agoraphobia, where I couldn't leave my room. Now, I run my own company, and I see friends, but I'm just a complete ghost. I have no memory of who I used to be. I feel as if I'm stuck in purgatory. Everything I loved, felt, experienced, or knew is gone. And I have no clue how I'm ever going to get it back."

As a therapist, hearing Mr. M's words reminded me that the body's attempt to protect us can sometimes become its own prison. When the dorsal vagal circuit takes over, it numbs the pain to help us survive, but in doing so, it also numbs the very things that make us feel alive.

This "prison" isn't just a mental state; it is a physical environment maintained by the body's internal chemistry. To understand why Mr. M feels so disconnected, we have to look at how our chemical messengers keep the nervous system stuck in these survival loops. Specifically, the hormones released by the endocrine system act as a feedback loop that directly affects the autonomic nervous system (ANS).

The primary hormones involved in this process are:

a) Cortisol, which is a stress hormone and is released *after* the sympathetic nervous system is activated, heightens the body's stress response and can increase feelings of stress and anxiety.

b) Oxytocin, which is a hormone associated with social bonding and relaxation, can support states linked to ventral vagal activation, promoting feelings of safety and calm.

The polyvagal theory helps us see that our body's state and our emotions are a two-way street. Our physiological state influences hormone levels, and hormone levels, in turn, feed back into our emotional experience.

When the sympathetic nervous system is activated (e.g., due to stress or danger), it triggers the release of stress hormones like cortisol. This, in turn, can influence mood and emotional responses. When the ventral vagal complex is active (promoting calm and social engagement), it can decrease stress hormones and increase hormones associated with relaxation and social bonding. Our physiological state doesn't just reflect our emotions; it actively shapes them. For example, in a stressful situation, the endocrine system releases hormones that affect the ANS, potentially increasing sympathetic activation and influencing our emotional responses. By contrast, environments perceived as safe, the ventral vagal system can dominate, promoting a calm state and possibly leading to reduced stress-hormone activity that support positive emotions and social interactions.

Understanding how these systems interact can help in therapeutic settings. For instance, interventions that promote vagal tone (e.g., deep breathing exercises and social engagement) can help manage stress and improve hormonal balance, leading to better emotional regulation. Now, let's learn how to work with our emotions directly.

Many experiences leave a lasting mark on us. While the specific details may fade, the feeling of the moment often remains clear and potent. We're going to take time to carefully access those powerful emotional memories.

Imagine your brain as a bustling city where emotions are like fireworks lighting up the skyline. These emotional sparks set off a cascade of feel-good chemicals in your brain's pleasure centers and activate neural networks across the brain that integrate both analytical and creative processing. Instead of one side "handling logic" and the other "handling creativity," your entire brain engages dynamically, as if your emotions were hosting a celebration and inviting every system to participate.

Dealing With Strong Emotions

Positive Emotions

Positive emotions are beneficial for both the mind and body. They strengthen coping mechanisms, contributing to overall well-being. This, in turn, can increase motivation to achieve goals and provide satisfaction as we progress.

Let's look at an example. Ms. S received an increment and was promoted to a managerial post, where she had worked for a long time. Since this was big news, her close-knit friends persuaded her to join them at a nearby club to celebrate. As she entered, the blaring music sent a surge of excitement through her body, her bloodstream responding with the natural rush of heightened arousal rather than fear-driven adrenaline. She looked at her friends, each of them celebrating her long-awaited promotion as they huddled together in the club. Her heart pulsed in rhythm with the deep bass of a newly released pop single. Her eyes brightened with joy, and her cheeks flushed even without makeup. She hadn't felt so thrilled in a long time.

We all have these touchstone memories, experiences that leave a permanent, vivid mark. Milestones such as forming meaningful relationships, celebrating achievements, or welcoming new responsibilities may evoke such emotional clarity. You may feel similar emotions when bringing home a pet, like a puppy, when it looks at you in all its innocence. Or recall celebratory moments, like when you graduated and embarked on a new phase of life. It is also possible to experience this through reconnecting with nature in ways you hadn't before. Spending time outdoors, such as camping or exploring forests, can surface emotions tied to wonder, calm, and connection. These aren't just events; they are emotional landmarks that shape how we see the world and navigate our lives.

To reconnect with that feeling, engage your senses. Listen to a song that takes you back to that moment. Buy that same cologne you wore at special times. Use sensory cues to help your mind access the emotional memory with greater clarity.

What experiences have made you feel most alive?

Negative Emotions

In response to our thoughts, our brain releases hormones and chemicals. These chemicals send us into a state of arousal.

Our brain translates our thoughts into chemistry, releasing hormones that drive our emotional state. All emotions, whether positive or negative, arise in this way. While positive emotions lift us, negative ones often overwhelm us, and we aren't always taught how to navigate them well. Unfortunately, life can also take a turn for the worse, and we are forced to go through bad experiences that leave us feeling so discouraged that progress seems out of reach.

Prolonged negative emotion does more than just hurt, it reduces the brain's ability to stay open, flexible, and receptive, making it difficult to work through issues and be the best versions of ourselves. These emotions can distort perception, casting a shadow over everything we perceive.

Consider Mr. B's story: Mr. B was never going to be the same again. He had just been through a breakup and was experiencing mixed feelings of sadness and denial. He was feeling ashamed of himself because he was not able to make it "work out" for him. He had been an ambitious person who had never let failure cross his path. However, his unsuccessful relationship broke him to the core and intensified emotions that began affecting every area of his life. He was lacking badly in his professional life as well. His boss called him into the office yesterday and confided in him about the prospective opportunity coming along the way soon. The company was going to send a crew, and Mr. B might be chosen to lead it. The most surprising factor in this entire situation was his substandard performance during recent months. After what he had gone through, he had not been the energetic and driven Mr. B who had joined the company three years earlier. Nonetheless, his boss had assured him of the potential he believed Mr. B still had. Mr. B's negative emotions were now threatening his future.

This is a common pattern. Life throws countless opportunities our way, and we, remaining huddled up in our shells of desolation and self-doubt, let each of them pass by with our weary eyes. Some of us succeed in making the most out of circumstances with their discovered secret. They discover a kind of key—not a magic formula, but a shift in perspective that allows them to transform their hardships into strength. For those who have already instilled this approach within their lives, kudos to you!

Propounding Dichotomy

Alright, no more suspense. This isn't a secret code to crack. In fact, it's quite simple. Think of it as a fundamental fork in the road. According to this principle, whenever something undesirable occurs in our lives, we are met with several unconscious choices to make, which take us in two directions. One of these directions leads toward the path of success and fulfillment, the other toward failure and dejection. While we can't always control what happens to us, we can almost always steer our response.

I often tell people I work with this next part: what feels like a setback can actually be a setup for growth. When someone tells me, "My partner made me so mad," or shares an unwelcome experience, I walk them through how the moment itself can become a tool for self-development. So, if your partner was mad, you can use this opportunity to practice patience and validation and instill forgiveness. You can learn how to cope with someone else's overwhelming emotions, or how to stay grounded without absorbing what they're expressing. So, I say welcome the opportunity. So, I say: welcome the challenge. See it as a training ground for your own peace.

- **Take a deep breath**
- **Protect your energy**
- **Use gratitude**
- **Utilize a song or positive vibrations**

Remind yourself that it's not yours; it's their issue

Is it easy? No. But it is possible.

When your spirit feels low and negative emotions are hard to shake, start gently. Look back at what you've already overcome. Remember a time you felt strong and capable—let that memory re-ignite the feeling. We can't always have cheerleaders around us. In those moments, you learn to become your own source of encouragement. Reconnect with yourself. Recall your own resilience. This is how you rebuild an unshakable belief in yourself.

Which accomplishments of yours have contributed the most to your growth? In what ways do you think they have shaped who you are today?

You should feel proud of how far you have come. These achievements not only add value to your life but also help boost your self-confidence and support the development of new strengths. Now, I don't want you to be stuck in the past and cherish that; I want you to make new memories and do something new. I want you to make your time here on earth worthwhile. So, move forward and embrace what life has in store for you.

Art of Moving Forward

Who doesn't feel a wave of nostalgia remembering their first bicycle race or a childhood lemonade stand? We all cherish our early years, and even those who have endured and experienced some of the most traumatic incidents of their lives take pleasure in recalling the sense of freedom our younger selves went through. Taken care of, and without a worry of what's to come, several defining facets of our personalities are formed during our childhood. This time of life has more significance in shaping our minds and ideas than we realize.

But if moving forward is the goal, why look back? Because revisiting positive memories isn't about dwelling in the past; it's about fueling the present. But holding on to the events and incidents that you cherish and treasure creates an optimistic imprint within your mind and emotional patterns. If you are sure not to let it get the best of you and avoid getting stuck replaying the same moment out of nostalgia, it only works in your best interests.

Through research, it has been learned that recalling a happy memory not only boosts your confidence but also makes you more optimistic in any situation. So, when you intentionally revisit these joyful incidents and bring them back into your active memory, you boost your self-esteem and strengthen your connection with your own identity.

A simple way to practice this is to keep reminders of good times around you; hanging photos of happy memories around the house, souvenirs, or music from happy periods can serve as instant portals to those feelings. Used wisely, nostalgia is a tool, not a trap.

Let's do a happy memory recall exercise together. Let's take it back to the beginning, your childhood!

What made you happy as a child?

Now, write down all the things you have the utmost belief in yourself of accomplishing ahead in life.

I believe I can...

____

____

____

____

____

____

____

____

Mission Statement

Every business that ever existed had its own mission statement to set the path ahead. A strong mission statement helps establish the direction your business or company is headed and what it aims to do, which ultimately determines success.

But what if you applied the same principle to your own life? A personal mission statement isn't corporate jargon; it's a compass built from your deepest values. Everything you aim for and achieve stems from what you truly believe matters. This statement keeps you aligned, reminds you of your "why," and grounds you in your integrity. Now, ask yourself, "Would it be better if, instead of letting my subconscious mind take hold of me and my decisions, I consciously take control of my life?" The answer is yes. Start by defining your core values. What is it that you deem important? What are those things that add meaning to your existence? Indulge a little deeper in these queries and then commit to the exercise below in creating your own personal mission statement.

Let me help you get started with an example of my own personal mission statement. "My mission is to bring awareness to people that they aren't alone in this world. There are people who will listen, people who care, and people who will be there for them. I never want anyone to feel alone or helpless. My mission is to be available to help and to change the stigma of talking to a therapist about issues to encourage people to be vulnerable in order to get their needs met."

What is your mission?

Let's create your personal mission statement

Let's create your professional statement

Now that you have created your mission statements, let's incorporate them into your life. Some people get it framed, save it as a screensaver, or simply write it on a post-it and stick it on their refrigerator. Find what works best for you. Have fun with it! This will be your new best friend who's there to remind you to stay true to your values, goals, who you are, and who you want to be.

Notes for Chapter 2

Key Takeaways

- **The most important person in your life is yourself.**
- **Familiarize yourself as if you were a stranger.**
- **Get to know more about yourself by reflecting on your accomplishments.**
- **Reflecting back on pleasant memories and indulging in activities that bring you happiness, such as your hobbies, can make you feel more optimistic.**
- **Your mission statement decides the trajectory of moving ahead in life with a concrete vision.**
- **Take care of yourself: Just like on an airplane, it is important to put on your oxygen mask first and then help others. It is also important to help yourself before you go out to help someone else.**

Chapter 3: Really, Who is The Person in The Mirror?

We give the universe its meaning. Everything exists because we are here to experience and observe it. From the celestial bodies floating in the space-time continuum to the microcosmic nature of subatomic particles, in a very real sense, the world exists because you are here to perceive it.

And despite this apparent reality staring us in the face every day, our mind is led astray when we center our concerns and worries on everything that isn't us. The urge is too strong and the distraction too powerful. We do everything for ourselves, yet we avoid truly seeing ourselves. From acquiring material comforts to making justifications for the mistakes made in the past, our subconscious remains affixed to attending to our own needs and wants.

But doesn't this create a paradox? Of course, it does. The way through is to turn our conscious attention inward. A simple lesson in psychology will tell you how our subconscious is formed through consciousness. Therefore, it becomes of primary importance that we always work on the latter first to change our thought patterns. To begin with this change, let's conduct a simple exercise. Stand in front of a mirror alone.

Begin a conversation, look deep into your eyes, and spend some time with your thoughts. Try to stay away from any distractions as you do this. Find a quiet moment and eliminate all distractions. Turn off music, television, and podcasts. Let the only sound be your own breath, the only focus is your own reflection. Practice this for fifteen minutes.

Write down what you experienced.

Rate how comfortable this was for you.

(1 = extremely uncomfortable, 10 = extremely comfortable)

1 2 3 4 5 6 7 8 9 10

More often than not, we worry about our perception in someone else's mind. In my work as a therapist, I have seen people anxious, depressed, and undermining their personal growth in fear of being judged or perceived in a negative manner. Whether it's a natural instinct or not isn't important; what's important is that it affects your growth and healing.

Of course, it will be too unrealistic to simply tell you not to care what others think. If it were that simple, wouldn't we all, somehow, have learned the art of being invincible against judgments?

The human mind is complex. We can't fully know why someone thinks the way they do or how they form their opinions, including their opinions of you. What's crucial to remember is that how someone sees you often says more about them than it does about you. They perceive you through the lens of their own experiences, biases, and capacity for understanding. If someone's view of you feels shallow or unfair, it may reflect their limitations, not yours. Does that mean it was you who couldn't make yourself discernible enough? No.

In psychology, impression management is about how therapists deal with how people perceive and react to them.

It's important because we're social creatures who need to handle criticism and feedback. Reputation management, on the other hand, is more about how we maintain our image over time. It's natural to want validation, but your sense of worth shouldn't be anchored in others' approval.

I once worked with a man I'll call Mr. T. He was a successful attorney in his mid-forties who appeared to have everything figured out. But in our sessions, I noticed something different.

"I've spent my entire adult life trying to meet everyone's expectations," he confessed. "My father wanted me in law because it was prestigious and lucrative, so I became a lawyer, even though I wanted to teach history. My wife wanted me to be more social and outgoing, so I forced myself to attend every networking event and dinner party, draining myself completely. My colleagues wanted me to be tougher, more aggressive in court, so I developed this persona that felt like wearing someone else's skin."

He looked directly at me and said, "What terrifies me is that when I look in the mirror, I can't find myself anywhere in there. I see my father's ambitions, my wife's social ideals, my firm's expectations. But me? The actual me? I don't know if he even exists anymore, or if he ever did."

Mr. T.'s eyes filled with tears. Surprisingly, it was the first genuine emotion I'd seen him express. "I'm forty-six years old, and I have no idea who I am when no one's watching."

In our therapy sessions, we focused on helping him learn to validate himself, rather than constantly seeking approval from others. It wasn't about rejecting others' input entirely, but about finding his own voice in the chorus of expectations. The first step was simply learning to recognize which thoughts were truly his own.

Use the following space for writing how you think others describe you

You may wonder why seeking validation or approval from others is important. Why does it even matter what someone else thinks of you? Wasn't the entire significance of a mindful culture rendered to "be yourself" and "not let judgments affect you"?

The key isn't to stop wanting approval entirely, but to become more mindful of its source. Yes, you need to be more open and mindful about where your approval is coming from and how it contributes to your overall growth. This is why the mirror exercise at the beginning of the chapter is so important; it helps you take the initial steps to validate yourself. In other words, these are also called positive affirmations. Let's have a look at what they can look like.

Examples of seeking validations:	Examples of seeking affirmations:
I seek validation that I'm a good partner	I'm a good partner
I need validation that I'm good at my job	I'm good at my job
I get validation by doing extra at work	I'm a hard worker
I do extra by sacrificing my own needs or feelings	I am a giving person I am a good person
I got a reward only by chance	I deserve this reward

Here, I want you to write your own:

Once you have affirmed yourself, no matter how small or large the achievement, create a strategy to reward that behavior. Our brains are wired to respond powerfully to rewards, which motivates us to repeat the actions that earned them. By pairing self-validation with a personal reward, you train your mind to work diligently toward your goals. It doesn't need to be something expensive. It could be a nap, a quiet walk in the park, a drive along the beach, or watching your favorite TV show/movie on streaming. You could reward yourself with an ice cream, a coffee, a manicure, or a spa treatment. Choose something that feels like a genuine gift to yourself.

This reinforcement works because of your brain's built-in reward system, involving areas like the nucleus accumbens and the prefrontal cortex. When we engage in activities that are essential for our survival or provide pleasure, such as eating, socializing, or engaging in sexual activity, the brain releases neurotransmitters like dopamine, serotonin, and endorphins. These chemicals create feelings of satisfaction and strengthen the neural pathways associated with the rewarding behavior, motivating you to do it again.

Moreover, these neurotransmitters not only create pleasure but also drive our motivation and desire for rewards. Also, none of us wants to die without leaving our mark behind. The curiosity of what people will say about us when we pass on catches everyone with its tentacles. I'm sure at one point, we've wondered how cool it would be to come back as a ghost to see how people remember us.

Therefore, we must address in a timely manner what is more valuable to us and, as I said before, transform undesirable events to work in our favor.

This idea can sound abstract until you see how it plays out in everyday life, especially in situations many of us recognize all too well. Most people have something they care deeply about but keep putting off, because something internal keeps getting in the way.

Let's look at an example from one of my clients, whom I'll refer to as Mr. L, to understand this more clearly.

Mr. L. is a writer who had been stuck for years. He'd been trying to finish a novel for almost three years, but his pattern never changed: he'd write intensely for a short time, then avoid it for weeks. During those breaks, he was hard on himself and felt like he was constantly falling behind.

He told me, "I've never really rewarded myself for anything. I always figured, 'Why would I reward myself for doing what I'm supposed to do?' And whatever I did never felt like enough. If I wrote one chapter, I thought I should have written two. If I finished a draft, I told myself it wasn't any good, so it didn't count."

We decided to try something simple. He would write for thirty focused minutes, then take a walk in a park he enjoyed.

The walk wasn't for thinking about the writing or judging how it went—it was just time to enjoy being outside.

At first, he didn't like the idea. "It feels unnecessary," he said. "Almost childish."

I pointed out that writing had become something he only associated with stress and self-criticism. The goal was to connect it with something that felt good instead.

Even though he was unsure, he gave it a try. About a month later, he noticed a change. Over time, writing stopped feeling like a punishment and started feeling manageable.

Four months later, he finished his novel.

Mr. L.'s experience shows how easily effort can become tangled with self-criticism, and how changing that relationship can quietly change everything. With that in mind, let's step back from productivity and consider a much bigger question.

Now, I want you to imagine you are dead, and everyone is gathered for your funeral.

What would you want people to say about you at your funeral? Let's write your eulogy. (I know it sounds a bit dark, but roll with it. Let's see what you come up with.)

____

____

____

____

Now, ask yourself, are you working towards becoming what you have mentioned above? Are you working towards all the goals that require being the person you want this eulogy to be read for?

It can be difficult, yes. But when you believe and then progress, no matter how slow the pace, you have established a promise, a guarantee, that achieving is possible.

Ask yourself, how do you want to be remembered, and what remnants do you want to leave behind? (Amuse me here!)

How do you feel after this thought-diving activity? (It's okay to practice being vulnerable here)

The purpose of this chapter and all the activities you have conducted will help you gain a sense of familiarity with yourself. Until you acquaint yourself with yourself, all your efforts may feel scattered or unfulfilling. If you're not working toward your goals from a place of personal fulfillment, you can easily lose your way.

Accepting yourself also comes with unraveling several layers of your existence. For example, you may begin to closely notice patterns such as your choice of a romantic partner, your inclination toward things, your reaction to different stimuli, and so on. Pursue this self-knowledge by continuing the reflective practices you've started here, and if you want to reinforce it, I would suggest you keep the feedback loop consistent and ongoing. Therefore, you can reenact these exercises in a separate journal once you have finished the book.

So, why is self-knowledge so important? It is the foundation that brings you closer to your authentic self, allowing you to refine and strengthen different parts of your personality. While it doesn't guarantee you'll avoid mistakes entirely, it helps you navigate life with more awareness, making errors less frequent and less severe.

Beyond that, self-knowledge boosts your social interactions and relationships. As a result, you merit high self-esteem and utmost self-belief, which strengthens your belief in yourself and the world around you.

Notes for Chapter 3

Key Takeaway

- **You are your own warrior and savior.**
- **Get acquainted with yourself on a regular basis by having conversations in the mirror.**
- **Your positive self-image is enhanced by the uplifting ways in which you believe others perceive you.**
- **Self-knowledge is a very important aspect in making you stronger and more confident as you go on accomplishing your goals.**
- **How others perceive you has a direct relationship with how you perceive yourself.**

Chapter 4: Uncovering Values & Emotions

Emotions are the crux of our existence. We are not merely intellectual beings. Our profound capacity to feel in multilayered ways sets us apart from other living beings in our evolutionary lineage. From a scientific point of view, emotions are indeed the powerful drivers of our lives. They determine how we feel about people, things, and ourselves. They assign significance to our experiences, shape our life goals, and influence our will to pursue them.

Observing an animal, we all have, at some point, wondered what makes us so different from, say, a cat or a dog. Don't animals, after all, consist of the very same biological machinery that keeps us running? We share similar organs and metabolic processes, yet something fundamental is different.

One could say that cognition and intelligence set us apart from all other mammals, if not all animals. They typically do not lament their existence or wrestle with existential dread, living more squarely in the here and now. If that's the case, is our supposed superiority based solely on intellectual prowess? Is that the sole force behind all human achievement? The answer is no. Emotions control us in ways we often underestimate. Remember a time you felt enraged over something trivial, surprising even yourself? Or a moment when you were overwhelmed by grief and couldn't stop crying? They govern us in powerful, often unexpected ways, frequently taking the lead in our decisions. Whether we're sad, happy, angry, or anxious, our emotions shape countless life choices. Our judgment, perspectives, and even our rational thinking are deeply influenced by our current emotional state.

Dr. Andrew Huberman, a neurobiologist from Stanford University, talks extensively about the science of emotions in his podcast, *Huberman Lab*. He explains how our behavior creates a feedback loop, creating a continuous circuit. Various neurotransmitters influence our susceptibility to specific emotional states. When we continuously expose ourselves to the triggers of our emotions, these chemicals help steer our feelings in a consistent direction.

Before we go further, let us understand how emotions affect our lives and why it is essential to recognize our emotional state of being. I'll also show you how acknowledging your feelings is a crucial step on the path to fulfillment you've begun with this book.

Let's begin with recognizing different emotions. Renowned American psychologist Paul Eckman proposed categorizing emotions into six distinct types, now widely accepted as the universal emotions.

Anger

Whether you call it fury, irritation, resentment, or outrage, we all experience anger within our personal capacity. Many things can fuel it, which is why people react at different intensities even to the same trigger. Some of the common reactions or responses emerging from anger are screaming, shouting, a hike in blood pressure, a pacing heart rate, decreased ability to focus/concentrate, or physical abuse in severe cases.

What makes a person angry is highly variable, and I am not here to tell you simply to "let it go." Trying to suppress anger is a common mistake. When you force emotions beneath the surface, they fester, consuming your inner peace like a hidden mold. What's important to notice here is that controlling your anger is different than suppressing it. Your goal should always be to maintain your anger within a harmless limit, rather than trying to subdue it beneath the surface. I teach a technique for this, which we will explore in the next chapter.

That said, it's okay to feel angry, but do not mistake this for a license to scream or inflict damage on others. Instead, I would urge you to learn to channel your emotions (more on this later in the chapter). Talk to your anger instead of ignoring it. Try this: Write a scene where you engage in a conversation with your anger. Visualize sitting across from this intense feeling, ready to address it. Acknowledge its presence and validate its reason for being, but be cautious not to dwell there too long.

Write a few words on what angers you the most.

____

____

____

____

____

____

____

Do some self-reflection, and write down how you react to anger in the space below.

____

____

____

____

____

____

____

Disgust

You know this feeling well: the extreme repulsion toward something that you don't even want to stay familiar with anymore. Like all the other emotions, what you feel disgusted about can vary according to your personal experiences or learning. For example, people suffering from OCD or germophobia may react with extreme disgust to a used hankie compared to others. The intensity of your disdain can dictate your future actions. In modern terms, we often call this feeling "cringe." If I have one piece of advice, it's this: try to understand the origin of your disgust. Examining or intellectualizing an emotion can be a powerful tool for processing trauma or uncovering its roots. This practice can also be your first step toward understanding your broader emotional responses to various triggers.

Write a few lines about what disgusts you the most. How does it leave you feeling? Where did it originate from?

Fear

As part of our flight, fight, or freeze response, fear has had a significant evolutionary role for human beings. Yet, as we've evolved from primal life, this powerful emotion can often hinder more than help. For example, think about why the thought of someone pointing a gun at you scares you so much. Or the fear of heights. It all originates from our desire to ensure our survival. Fear is our reaction when we feel endangered. However, in our modern world, these deep-rooted fears can stunt our growth and prevent us from making decisions leading to a fulfilled life.

Fear could directly stem from earlier life traumas, When these unresolved experiences shape our present selves, we may question our own capabilities. There are countless variations as to how one could feel afraid of certain things. For example, you might know someone afraid of commitment. Never hesitate to ask *why* when confronting fear. Why were they afraid? Maybe he, she, or they had been through a rough breakup; perhaps they lost their trust in someone they loved; maybe they had observed an abusive relationship with their parents growing up.

A woman I worked with, let's call her Ms. L., a talented graphic designer in her early thirties, repeatedly sabotaged herself just as major opportunities appeared. She'd been missing deadlines, canceling interviews, and even deleting finished work. "I watch myself ruin everything. It's like I can't stop," she said.

As we explored her history, the pattern became clear. Growing up, success was never celebrated. Every achievement was met with raised expectations and the threat of disappointment. Straight A's became "the new baseline." Awards became pressure. Praise was replaced with impossible standards.

Over time, she learned that success led to loss of safety, approval, and room to breathe. Sabotage became protection. If she failed first, no one could tear her down afterward.

We focused on separating her mother's voice from her own and redefining success as something that didn't automatically demand more. When she finally completed a major project without self-sabotage, she took herself out to dinner to mark the moment.

"No one raised the bar," she told me later. "It didn't turn sour. It was just... good."

You can apply a similar process to trace your own fears to their roots. Even better, consider working with a therapist to explore them, especially if they feel overwhelming, or when you're simply ready to move through your fears and grow.

What scares you the most?

____

____

____

____

____

____

____

Happiness

We are often led to believe our entire existence depends on the pursuit of happiness, that it is life's ultimate goal, and every endeavor should maximize our well-being. We all strive for it. Everyone wants to be happy. While we may never agree on a universal recipe for bliss, we can acknowledge that our pursuits are often tied to gaining pleasure or satisfaction.

Our brains release neurotransmitters in response to specific stimuli, creating that "butterflies-in-the-stomach" feeling—whether from talking to a loved one, making a purchase, or winning a game.

However, this feeling is fleeting. There often comes a time when the same stimulus no longer brings the same joy. Have you wondered why your partner doesn't spark that same intense excitement? What we often mistake for happiness is simply our neurochemistry at work, which can obscure what true, lasting fulfillment means. Imagine if our brains had two switches: one for instant pleasure and another for delayed gratification. The second switch, delayed gratification, promotes longer-lasting satisfaction. This is because it triggers the release of chemicals like serotonin and endorphins, which create deeper, more sustained feelings of well-being.

What brings you the most pleasure? How do you feel when it happens?

This is also how addiction operates within our nervous system, driven by the same reward pathways. Drugs or alcohol hijack the brain's reward system by flooding the nucleus accumbens with excessive dopamine, creating a powerful compulsion for more.

Sadness

Sadness moves through us in many forms: melancholy, nostalgia, desolation, dejection, and countless shades of the same core emotion. Whether it's the death of a loved one, a breakup, or even the closing of a favorite restaurant, we have all felt its weight. It is also one of the most intense emotions, with the ability to linger for a prolonged period of time. Its power can overshadow joy and pull us into hopelessness. Unlike other emotions, there cannot be an instant remedy to overcome deep sadness. My suggestion to you will be to try intellectualizing your emotions because when you do that, you are making sense of your sadness through rational reasons.

Let's say someone experiences a breakup and feels deeply saddened by it. Instead of allowing themselves to fully feel and process the emotions associated with the breakup, they might intellectualize their sadness by rationalizing it with reasons such as:

- **"The relationship wasn't healthy anyway."**
- **"We had irreconcilable differences."**
- **"Now I can focus on my own growth."**
- **"Breakups are a natural part of life."**

In this scenario, rather than confronting and experiencing the raw emotions of heartbreak and sadness, the individual attempts to make sense of their feelings by analyzing the situation logically and providing rational explanations for why they feel the way they do. While intellectualizing can provide temporary relief or clarity, it can also block the full processing and healing necessary to move forward. That's why, as you try this, I also advise you to consciously embrace your sadness. Sit with it in solitude for a moment. Invite it in and have a kind conversation. Talk to your sadness instead of ignoring it. Do not judge yourself for feeling this way, or you may start a downward spiral. Acknowledge its presence with respect, but be mindful not to linger there too long.

List of Other Holistic Things to Try When Sad

1. Practice mindfulness
2. Listen to upbeat music or access a sound bath
3. Use touch (can lower cortisol and increase oxytocin)
4. Include Omega-3 fatty acids in your diet
5. Stop the negative self-talk
6. Bide your time (remind yourself that change is constant and that you won't always feel this way)
7. Distract yourself (from overthinking)
8. Have a doctor check your vitamin D levels: get more light
9. Therapy (CBT)
10. Keep a journal

11. Connect with uplifting friends and family
12. Get exercise, and start taking daily or nightly walks
13. Get enough sleep
14. Forgive yourself and forgive others
15. Daily positive affirmations
16. Reward yourself when you accomplish something
17. Don't give up, be kind and gentle with yourself
18. Eat a healthy, nutrient-rich diet
19. Watch an upbeat movie
20. Try to laugh, smile more at others, and your reflection
21. Change your environment; go on a vacation, leave your town for a new atmosphere

Intrusive thoughts are often the cause of our sadness. More often, they originate from our traumas or a momentary, unfavorable incident. When thoughts like these take over and cast the feeling of sorrow, it is better to deal with them through rational reasoning or, in other words, by intellectualizing.

What do you do when you feel sad? Write down the things that trigger most of your unhappy episodes.

____

____

Surprise

This emotion ranges from a sudden startle to the shock of unmet expectations. Anything that our mind does not understand could exist and surprise us. Think for a minute about what would happen if something started hovering in the air instead of falling under the force of gravity. Would you not be surprised?

Think of a child's face at a magic show when the magician pulls a rabbit from a hat. Recall your own moments of wonder, from childhood to now, as the sources of your surprise have evolved.

While surprise may not impact us as deeply as other emotions, it's important to acknowledge. People react to it differently, some love surprises, others dread them. Consider your own preference. Have you wondered why? Our liking or disliking of surprise is shaped by our personal history and how our brain has learned to respond to the unexpected.

When was the last time you found yourself startled? How did it make you feel?

____

____

____

____

____

____

____

These six basic emotions form the foundation for the complex feelings that shape our daily experience. Consider a moment of surprise. Was the cause joyful, like a surprise party, or terrifying, like a confrontation with a burglar?

Complex emotions arise from the interplay and overlap of these basic feelings. For instance, recall a time you felt both sad and angry simultaneously. This blend creates a unique emotional state. This principle applies universally; when our core emotions intersect, they generate nuanced responses and behaviors to life's varied stimuli.

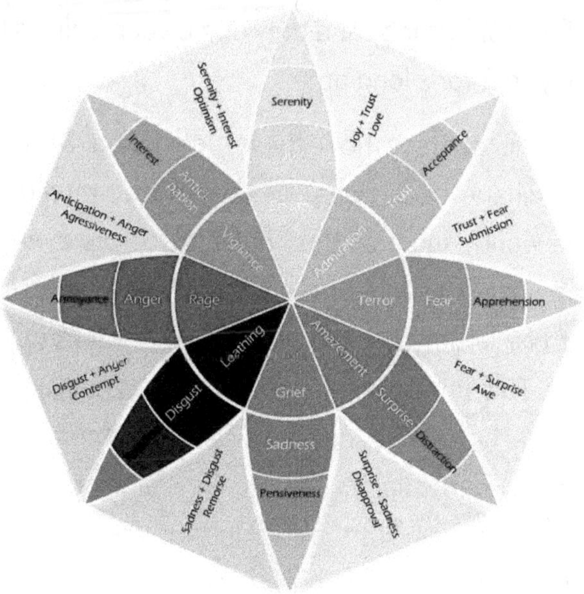

Figure 4.1: The Wheel of Emotions[5]

Figure 4.1 illustrates these emotions. Looking closely, you'll see the wheel includes two additional core emotions: trust and anticipation. In therapy, these hold significant weight. Trust is a mental construct that reinforces our belief in someone's or something's dependability. In relationships, it provides the confidence and security needed to move forward. Anticipation, however, can be positive or negative, shaped entirely by expectation. Recall waiting for your final grades. This emotion also deeply influences social behavior. For example, if you hope your partner will plan something

[5] Mondal, Abhijit & Gokhale, Swapna. (2020). Mining Emotions on Plutchik's Wheel. 1-6. 10.1109/SNAMS52053.2020.9336534.

special for your birthday and they don't, your feelings toward them may shift for a long time.

Now you can see how these underlying feelings and reactions shape your behavior in various situations. You might be wondering how this connects to your overall state of being—specifically, your emotional well-being. Clarity comes from understanding the root and intensity of your emotions. This understanding is the first step in untangling the potential harm they may have caused in your life. Such a strategy is particularly useful for changing persistent behavioral patterns. Start by asking yourself: Have I been stuck with the same problem for a long time? If so, reflect on the recurring mistakes you've made, wondering how you keep ending up in the same place.

And now, let us have a look at the chart below to further understand your emotions and their origin. Again, I need you to take your sweet time in filling out the spaces while thinking as deeply as you can. This process may take you down memory lane, recalling experiences from your earlier years. Try to remember the farthest back you can recall seeing someone express anger. Did their anger spark your own? Consider this: if you hadn't been near that person, would you have developed the same emotional response?

In the table's second column, labeled "origin," note where you believe this emotion first took root in you. Do you wish to change this pattern? If yes, mark the third column and explain why. Use the space at the end of the chapter if you need more room.

For each emotion, write your personal description of it. Bring to mind a specific memory linked to that feeling. For the origin, explain where and when you felt it most strongly. You can use the extra pages at the chapter's end for longer reflections.

Dr. Brené Brown, a leading researcher and professor at the University of Houston, emphasizes the critical importance of coping with the adversity within us—what she often refers to as our "negative" emotions, which can cause long-term damage if unaddressed.

She explores the deep connection between our emotions and cognitive functions like reasoning, logic, and decision-making, showing how our feelings directly steer our thought processes. Dr. Brown underscores that when we process our emotions in a healthy way, they become a source of resilience and hope, paving the way to a more fulfilled life. This next step involves witnessing your darker, often hidden emotions, a practice known as "shadow work." Confronting this inner shadow deepens self-awareness, fosters growth, and reveals parts of yourself that usually remain concealed. Think of shadow work as a form of self-guided psychotherapy, allowing you to approach feelings you may have ignored or never fully recognized.

The concept was developed by psychologist Carl Jung to describe the traits we suppress or refuse to acknowledge, often perceived as negative. However, Jung believed this practice could unlock buried positive qualities, such as creativity and innovation. By exploring our shadow, we better understand our place in the world and, in Jung's view, move toward greater balance and wholeness.

Here's what it can look like to uncover hidden aspects of yourself before attempting the exercise.

Mr. A., a project manager in his forties, came to therapy for "stress management," but quickly revealed a pattern of intense irritation toward others. He was an arrogant coworker, an attention-seeking neighbor, a controlling brother. The people changed, but the reaction didn't.

When I asked him to describe his father, he said, "Brilliant. He's a surgeon. Also arrogant, domineering, always had to be right. I hated that. I swore I'd never be like him."

Over time, it became clear that the traits Mr. A. most despised in others were the ones he'd disowned in himself. He, too, wanted recognition. He, too, felt pride in his expertise, but labeled those impulses "confidence" or "leadership" in himself and "arrogance" in others.

This was his shadow he'd buried because they reminded him of his father. Through our work, he learned he could integrate those traits without becoming the man he resented.

He could be confident without being domineering and ambitious without diminishing others.

Months later, he told me how the internal judgment had lifted.

"The people haven't changed, but I have. The things I hated most in others were the things I needed to make peace with in myself."

This is exactly what you need to do. With that in mind, we can now turn inward and begin the same process of recognition and integration for yourself.

Now it's your turn to apply this lens to your own inner world.

In the table below, we've listed several emotions. Your task is to trace the origin of each: How did you acquire this emotional response? Who might you have learned it from? Ask yourself whether your reactions are authentically yours or adopted from others, shaped by beliefs or past experiences. Then, determine if the emotion serves you in a healthy way and decide whether to keep it or work to change it.

Remember, emotions are normal, necessary, and inevitable. What matters is *how* we feel them, internalize them, and choose to respond. Keep in mind that emotions also function as an internal alarm system, signaling when something is off and prompting us to evaluate our health, surroundings, and relationships.

Emotions	Learning/ conditioning What does it look like for you? How did you pick this up from someone? What shaped this response?	Keep it or Change
Joy		
Disgust		
Anticipation		
Fear		
Sadness		
Disgust		
Surprise		
Trust		
Anger		
Love		
Disappointment		
Support		

Safety/Security		
Helplessness		
Obsession		
Infatuation		
Rage		
Bitter		
Critical		
Ambitious		
Prepared		
Frustrated		

Once you are done with ascertaining these emotions:

Make a list of past triggers, dig into them, and discover your shadow. (Get to the root)

Make a list of traits in others that trigger you to look into yourself. (Projection)

Make a list of things we judge in other people.

The point is to listen to them subconsciously and then play them out in our conscious mind. Let's try assimilating a bit of the shadow: This should lead to self-acceptance and self-forgiveness.

Exercise: Accepting the existence of your shadow.

What qualities and intentions are you aware of in your shadow self?

Now, let's try integrating the shadow. This will bring your hidden parts from your subconscious to your conscious mind. Being aware of them, including the good and the bad.

Exercise: Question the projections that you discovered above. Roleplay, have a conversation with your shadow aspects, or if you'd like, write a letter to this shadow self.

Completing the shadow. What's suppressed will come out. Suppressing the subconscious part of the psyche, parts of us that make us ashamed and make our presence worse.

Exercise: Consciously acknowledge your feelings (even if you don't want to express or act on them).

Visualize yourself from a different perspective; imagine yourself in front of someone who makes you feel uncomfortable or even insecure. Try to see yourself from their point of view.

Why did you want to hide these?

Who told you to suppress these parts of yourself? (parents, classmates, internet)

How true is it that people won't like you if you show these traits?

Now that you have familiarized yourself with your emotions, their origins, and your will to change certain emotional responses and accept your shadow self, let us move to the next step.

What you are unaware of, you cannot begin to control.

Accepting your shadow allows you to change, to understand yourself, and to find your balance.

> NOTE: If you suffer from Depersonalization-Derealization Disorder or Dissociative-Identity Disorder, please skip this part

This part of the chapter involves giving your emotions distinct identities. As an example, let me describe what my anger looks like when I personify it. My angry persona, "Raquel," wears a black leather jacket with studded pants and heavy boots. Her hair is spiked and dyed pink, her eyes are lined dramatically, and her lips are a deep, dark shade. She is short-tempered and confrontational, and her brow is permanently furrowed.

Giving an identity to an emotion helps us understand its role in our lives. Personification allows us to examine feelings from a new perspective. For instance, Raquel's permanent scowl reflects how anger can isolate me from my surroundings.

Every detail of her appearance reveals something about that emotion's nature. Before you begin, consider what a specific emotion evokes for you. What comes to mind with the word "happy"? Perhaps a vivid childhood memory. Note the colors, sensations, and images it brings up. Use those details to design the "costume" and demeanor of your emotion's persona.

And now, in the space below, describe the personality of each of your emotions.

Happy:

Sad:

Angry:

Surprised:

Afraid:

What do we achieve from this? Familiarity. The purpose of this chapter is to help you value your emotions by recognizing them as part of you, even the ones that hurt. See them not as your entire identity, but as contributors to your whole self. Our emotions shape us, and rather than denying or ignoring them, we must learn to embrace, understand, and respond to them wisely.

In your quiet moments, make peace with your feelings. Invite them in. Welcome them to sit and talk. Whether it's deep sadness or rising anger, tell your emotions you are present with them, offering reassurance. As I've said, neglecting emotions often intensifies them, making it harder to acknowledge and process what you truly feel. Therefore, learn to embrace and honor them. Be your own best friend or your own therapist when you need one.

For example, when I feel angry, I close my eyes and imagine Raquel beside me. I start a conversation: "Hey

Raquel, what's going on?" This opens a channel where I can engage with the emotion, offer it guidance, and still remain grounded in my rational mind (the frontal cortex). In this way, I care for my inner world without letting the emotion fully take over. Feel free to try this for yourself.

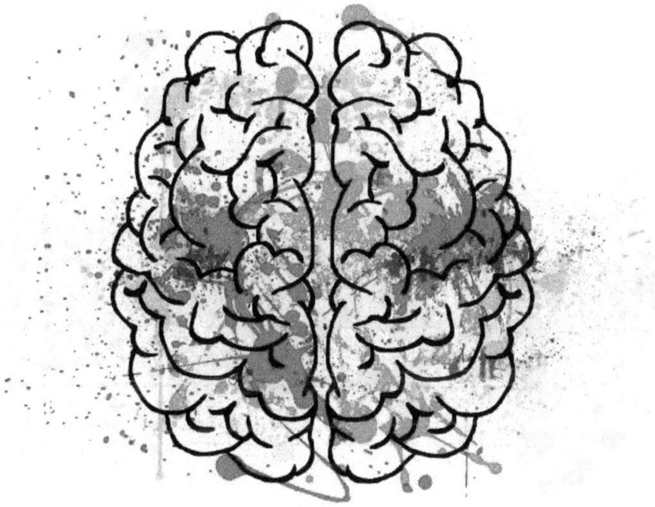

Notes for Chapter 4

Key Takeaway

- **Our e*motions* control a significant part of our lives and are responsible for most of the decisions we make throughout our day.**
- **Our emotions or reactions often originate and are associated with, mostly, earlier parts of our lives.**
- **There are six basic emotions, further expanded into eight emotions as given in the table.**
- **These basic emotions expand into further complex emotions, defining our responses and reactions to things.**
- **Associating identities with our emotions helps us bring ourselves closer to them and understand them from an entirely altered perspective. This also allows us to help ourselves.**

Chapter 5: Facing Our Individual Pain: Internalized Troubles

NOTE TO THE READER: IF THIS PART IS TOO INTENSE, YOU MAY NEED TO STOP AND SEEK TRAUMA TREATMENT FROM A LICENSED TRAUMA THERAPIST.

In this chapter, we will look more deeply at one of the most challenging aspects of human experience: trauma. Definitions and understandings of trauma can vary widely. My aim is to explain it from a psychological perspective so you can recognize its different forms, both harmful and less severe, and know when to seek support.

Simply put, trauma is a psychological response to a deeply distressing or disturbing event. But not all trauma is the same. Psychologists often categorize it into two broad types:

- **Complex Trauma**
- **Uncomplicated Trauma**

Complex trauma is a more intricate and pervasive form of psychological injury. It results from prolonged or repeated exposure to traumatic events, often within relationships or environments where escape feels difficult or impossible. Examples include ongoing childhood abuse, chronic domestic violence, repeatedly witnessing violence, forced cultural relocation, or surviving in a war zone. The effects of complex trauma are profound, often reshaping a person's personality, relationships, and fundamental worldview.

Uncomplicated trauma, which is also known as single-incident trauma, typically results from a one-time, unexpected event. This could be a car accident, a natural disaster, sexual assault, or witnessing a violent act. The effects of uncomplicated trauma, while potentially severe, are usually more straightforward to identify and treat. Individuals experiencing uncomplicated trauma may exhibit symptoms such as flashbacks, nightmares, or heightened anxiety related to the specific incident. With proper support and intervention, many people can process and recover from uncomplicated trauma over time.

It is important to note that complex trauma often occurs during critical developmental periods, fundamentally shaping a person's core beliefs about themselves and others. It can lead to a range of symptoms beyond those typically associated with post-traumatic stress disorder (PTSD), including difficulties with emotional regulation, interpersonal relationships, and even one's sense of identity.

Understanding the distinction between these two types of trauma is crucial for several reasons. First, it helps in accurate diagnosis and appropriate treatment planning. Second, it allows individuals to comprehend their own experiences and reactions better. Lastly, it guides society in developing more nuanced and effective trauma prevention and intervention approaches. Now that we are exploring our past and looking at our present selves, let's have a difficult conversation. Our target here is not to point the finger outward or assign blame, but instead, to be realistic and honest with ourselves. We will be unearthing past hurts and examining their impact. However, I want to clarify that our focus is not on the "why" of your traumas. If you need to go through the structured stages of trauma and healing, please seek therapy to properly address them.

Herman (1992) identifies three core stages of trauma recovery: safety, mourning, and reconnection.[6] Following these, many individuals also process trauma through the traditional five stages of grief (Kübler-Ross, 1969).[7] Here are a few stages you go through during or after experiencing a traumatic event:

- ***<u>Stabilization and safety.</u> Following the traumatic event, you may find yourself withdrawing from others...***

[6] Herman, J. L. (1992). Trauma and Recovery. Basic Books.
[7] Kübler-Ross, E. (1969). On Death and Dying. Macmillan

- ***Mourning and Remembrance.*** ***During this stage, you'll begin to create your own answers to the question, "What does all this mean?"***
- ***Integration and reconnection.*** ***It is important to go through the grief after trauma with a professional.***
- ***Denial*** ***– this can't be happening.***
- ***Anger*** ***– why did this have to happen?***
- ***Bargaining*** ***– I promise I'll never ask for another thing if only you will...***
- ***Depression*** ***– a gloom that comes from having to adjust to so much so quickly.***
- ***Acceptance*** ***With that being said, we're simply going to focus on being stuck after receiving trauma treatment or after a negative situation or a less traumatic situation to get unstuck, heal, and move forward.***

When you get stuck on the "why," it becomes easier to make excuses and allow yourself or the trigger to control the situation. A trigger occurs because your brain never fully registered that the danger has passed. So, you remain on high alert, hypervigilant, and reactive even when it's unnecessary.

Everyone can relate to that moment after an alarming experience, left questioning why you had to endure such pain. The "why me" feeling is universal, and frankly, no one wants to repeat it. What's important to understand is that adopting a "victim" mindset can become a trap, leaving us feeling too incapacitated to take the steps needed to overcome it.

What's wrong with the victim mentality, especially if you were truly victimized? It means you cling to that identity longer than is helpful and become dependent on it. The trauma doesn't just remain something that happened *to* you—it starts to define you. This often leads to avoiding solutions, feeling powerless, self-sabotage, low confidence, anger, and resentment. Remaining in this state long-term actually reinforces feelings of fear and lack of control.

A client I'll call Mr. P. came to therapy more than two years after a serious car accident that left him with chronic pain and a traumatic brain injury. Physically, doctors said he'd recovered as much as expected. Emotionally, he was still living at the intersection where it happened.

Everyone told him to move on, but the accident had cost him his job, strained his marriage, and pulled him away from friends, hobbies, and exercise. "How am I supposed to move forward when my life feels ruined?" he asked.

His accident gave him a reason for why his life had stalled and protected him from facing uncomfortable realities that predated the crash: a job he already hated, a struggling marriage, depression, and withdrawal. This was the paradox of the victim identity. Mr. P. had truly been victimized, but remaining "the accident victim" felt safer than risking failure without something external to blame. "If I try again and fail," he said, "then it's on me."

Our work focused on separating what happened to him from who he was. Slowly, he began to reclaim parts of himself—coaching his daughter's soccer team, reconnecting with his wife, playing guitar for ten minutes at a time.

"I still have pain," he told me later. "But I don't have to be defined by it. Being responsible for my life again is terrifying, but it's also more honest. And more hopeful than I ever expected." In our vocabulary, "hurt" is synonymous with damage. We can be hurt in countless ways, leaving us damaged, sometimes for a long time. Let's look at how people get hurt. Broadly, pain can be divided into tangible and intangible forms, with most emotional pain falling into the latter category.

Physical

This kind of tangible hurt varies in degree and can affect our bodies in various forms, from severe accidents causing paralysis to a simple bruise. It is almost always related to the physical body. Physical pain has its significance as a signal for us to seek a remedy. For example, if an injury didn't cause pain, you might not realize its severity or begin the recovery process.

Emotional

Though intangible, emotional pain can be one of the severest forms of hurt. It originates in various ways and, in many cases, leaves a deeper impact than physical injury. It can arise from someone else's actions or from experiences of loss, grief, and regret. It often brings a sense of hopelessness or disconnection from your surroundings.

Verbal

It may seem trivial, but verbal pain affects us more deeply than we often anticipate. Consider non-physical bullying as an example. In extreme cases, people can develop significant psychological distress from verbal abuse, even from those in their close circles. Verbal pain operates in direct opposition to appreciation and recognition and can affect your life profoundly. It can crush self-esteem so thoroughly that some people lose all confidence or stop believing in themselves entirely.

Fiscal

Financial hurt can result from a bad deal, a market crash, or a failed investment. This tangible loss can leave people deeply distressed and create a sense of hopelessness. To illustrate how severe this pain can be, consider the dramatic spike in suicides observed after the 2008 financial crisis.

Apart from these four basic types, the ways we can be hurt in life are endless. From career downfall to romantic rejection, we all face setbacks and heartache in different ways. What's more important is to recognize that what hurts one person may not hurt another to the same degree. Similarly, what traumatizes one may not be traumatizing to another.

But what determines the severity of our individual pain? Consider how long it takes some people to recover from the loss of a loved one. Or imagine if you and all your friends each lost ten thousand dollars. The emotional impact would vary widely for each person. From our initial reaction to how we process it, the trauma response is highly subjective. Let us now define trauma better. In simpler terms, psychological trauma is a "response to an event that a person finds highly stressful." Yet, it's important to note that not everyone who experiences the same stressful event will develop trauma. Everyone internalizes trauma differently. Let me share a personal example.

I went to NYC once. When I got out of the cab, I fell flat on my face in Times Square. My friends rushed to help, lifting me by my arms and legs until I was dangling awkwardly above the ground. In that moment, I felt like a fool, and this seemingly minor act of clumsiness was embarrassing to the point of feeling traumatic. But why?

Now, this incident may not have affected you with the same intensity or at all, and that's okay. We are all different, and our unique responses are valid. This is precisely why it is unhelpful and often harmful to compare or judge someone else's experience against your own. The neurobiology of trauma is rooted in the structure and function of our brain. Our brains function through electrical impulses called synapses, which are generated by neurons. When we face a traumatic situation, synaptic activity increases along specific neural pathways. These pathways are stored as memory, including the pattern of electrical signals. Each time you encounter a reminder, your brain reactivates this same pattern, and you re-experience the distress.

What is transgenerational trauma?

Transgenerational trauma refers to trauma that is passed from one generation to another. It can result from events such as war, genocide, oppression, or other forms of violence and adversity experienced by a community or family. Here are some steps to help heal its effects:

- ***Acknowledge and Understand*: Recognize that transgenerational trauma exists and understand its impact on individuals and families. Education and awareness are the keys to addressing and healing from it.**
- ***Therapy and Counseling:* Seek therapy or counseling from professionals specialized in treating this trauma. Therapy can provide a safe space to explore and process emotions, beliefs, and behaviors influenced by transgenerational trauma.**

- ***Family Support and Communication:*** **Foster open and supportive communication within the family. Encourage family members to share their experiences and emotions related to the trauma. Building connections and support networks can help in healing and breaking the cycle of trauma.**
- ***Cultural and Spiritual Practices:*** **Engage in cultural and spiritual practices that promote soothing and resilience. These practices could vary widely depending on cultural backgrounds but may include rituals, ceremonies, storytelling, and connecting with traditions.**
- ***Mindfulness and Self-Care:*** **Practice mindfulness techniques and prioritize self-care activities that promote emotional and mental well-being. Those could be meditation, yoga, journaling, exercise, and spending time in nature.**
- ***Break the Cycle:*** **Recognize the patterns of behavior and thoughts that may perpetuate the cycle. Challenge negative beliefs that have been passed down through generations.**
- ***Advocacy and Social Support:*** **Advocate for systemic changes that address the root causes of trauma and promote social justice and equity. Seek support from community organizations, advocacy groups, and mental health resources.**

Transgenerational trauma can have significant effects on individual and family systems. Open and honest communication can open up channels of healing and foster resilience amidst family adversity. Children of trauma survivors must be willing to work through their family's trauma to help break the cycle.

One of my clients, Ms. F's story, shows how trauma passes through generations and what breaking the cycle actually looks like in practice. Ms. F., a first-generation American in her early thirties whose parents had fled their country during a brutal civil war when they were in their twenties, came to therapy struggling with what she called *"inherited anxiety that makes no sense in my actual life."*

"My parents survived things I literally cannot imagine. They survived real trauma and actual war, displacement, loss of family members, persecution, and watching their friends disappear. They came to this country with two suitcases and $200. They worked three jobs each, learned a new language, and built a life from absolute nothing. They're heroes. I mean that genuinely, they are the strongest people I know. But they raised me in a state of constant, unrelenting fear. Never trust anyone outside the family, ever. The world is dangerous, always. Save every penny because disaster is always around the corner. Don't stand out, don't draw attention, don't take risks, don't trust institutions, don't relax, don't let your guard down for even a second. Stay hypervigilant every moment of every day because survival depends on it."

Growing up, Ms. F. had internalized these messages so completely that they felt like objective reality rather than her parents' trauma responses. Now, at thirty-two, she was paralyzed by anxiety despite living in relative safety and stability.

"I have panic attacks about things that aren't actually threatening. For instance, someone asks to see my ID at the bank, and I have a full panic attack. My heart races, and I can't breathe. Even when something good happens, instead of celebrating, I spend three days in terror that success will make me a target."

She couldn't enjoy things because she was always waiting for disaster. We talked about how children of trauma survivors often absorb their parents' hypervigilance and fear responses. Ms. F.'s parents had, with the best intentions, taught her to survive in a war zone she'd never actually lived in.

"You can carry forward their strength without carrying forward their fear," I told her.

Over time, Ms. F. learned to separate what still served her from what no longer did. The hypervigilance that once kept her parents alive in a war zone was creating anxiety in her peaceful life, and she realized she could honor their values without living in constant fear.

If you also feel yourself in a similar situation, it's time to break the cycle. Let us do some work now.

In the following space, write down who hurt you.

How did they hurt you?

How do you forgive them?

(AKA how you free yourself from anger and bitterness)

Note: Forgiveness has two sides: emotional and decisional forgiveness.

Emotional forgiveness allows one to no longer dwell on the choice to replace ill will with goodwill. Decisional forgiveness is one's conscious choice to replace ill will with goodwill.

For sure, maybe you can only do the emotional forgiveness for your sanity.

Now, if you had some trouble answering the last question, I need to tell you that you don't need to forgive someone; that's up to you, but forgiving yourself may be essential. The latter is most significant when you have been blaming yourself for the painful occurrence. Yes, despite wanting to, you cannot travel back in time and undo everything, so consider this: sit yourself down and have a talk.

Reflect on the mistakes you perceive, and then tell yourself out loud, "I forgive myself for that reaction I had that day," "I did the best I could," or "I am lovable." Keep in mind, we blame ourselves when we shouldn't. We need to release that blame from our shoulders. It's not your fault if you were abused, neglected, or mistreated.

Remember, healing often starts by reassessing where you place the blame. To understand how the body and brain respond during trauma, it helps to know a few key areas: the forebrain (prefrontal cortex), the limbic system (located in the center of the brain), and the brain stem. When a person experiences a traumatic event, adrenaline rushes through the body, and the memory is etched into the emotional memory center—the amygdala, which is part of the limbic system. The amygdala assigns emotional meaning to events and stores the trauma as sensory fragments: images, smells, sounds, tastes, or tactile sensations.

Here, we have usually trapped Negative Cognition about ourselves. Typically, it goes along the lines of:

- **I should' ve done something.**
- **I' m alone.**
- **I don' t trust anyone.**
- **I don' t trust myself.**
- **I should' ve known better.**
- **My best isn' t good enough.**
- **I am trapped.**
- **I am not in control.**
- **I cannot let it out.**
- **I am different.**
- **I am damaged.**

How we store our experiences is what sets the trajectory for us to move ahead. Every time we do not value ourselves, live inside a victim state, take responsibility for the traumatic experiences, and lack a sense of safety, choice and power, it will come to the surface! The following exercise may be a little hard to do right now, and I understand if you need to take a breather or skip this part altogether, all in your own time. You can come back to it later when you feel like you have recovered enough to have such difficult conversations with yourself.

What has traumatized you?

How were you traumatized?

What is your negative cognition attached to this event? (An 'I am' or 'I am not' statement)

____

____

____

____

____

____

____

How have these painful experiences affected you and still affect you today?

____

____

____

____

____

____

____

There is another fascinating exercise I often recommend. It carries deep symbolic weight, designed to help you internalize the relief that comes from closure.

Döstädning, or Swedish Death Cleaning, is a ceremonial practice where a deceased person's belongings are respectfully burned as a farewell. Far from being morbid, this ritual honors a spiritual transition, releasing both the person and their physical attachments. This act of transcendence can serve as a powerful metaphor for letting your own traumas depart through a personal ritual.

In this exercise, you will write a letter addressed directly to the person involved, as though they will read it. Channel all your emotions into it, using any tone that feels right. Once finished, you will ritually release it, burn it, tear it to shreds, or dispose of it in a way that feels meaningful. This practice parallels the intent of Swedish death cleaning, offering a tangible release.

Let's do another exercise: (Read through completely first, then close your eyes and begin). Close your eyes, revisit the experience, and imagine yourself at that younger age. Describe what you are wearing. What do the surroundings look like? (Picture your old house—the carpet, furniture, and artwork.) Visualize the scene in detail, but only if you feel emotionally safe to do so. What is happening? What is your younger self witnessing?

Now, step into the scene as your present-day adult self and provide what you needed at that time. Re-enact the event in your mind, this time offering the validation, strength, and support you lacked. In your imagination, tell your younger self, "You will be okay. You are perfect as you are." Offer the unconditional confidence they missed, and assure them that the future holds more than their current pain. In another psychological technique, you can use role-playing. This is safer to do with a therapist, as with all the techniques mentioned above, but if you feel safe, choose a trustworthy confidant and imagine they are the person connected to your trauma. Have a conversation with them, fully immersed, allowing yourself to believe you are speaking directly to that person. Let it all out. Tell them everything you deeply desire to say in a safe, trusting space.

This can help you find closure if you've been unable to speak to the actual person. Make sure your confidant is prepared to respond with kindness, offer validating statements, and participate in a supportive, healing way. It is helpful to guide them beforehand on how you would like them to respond.

And then, most importantly, meditate on it. I cannot stress enough how important the practice of meditation is for moving forward and recovering from your internalized troubles.

Meditate. Meditate. Meditate.

Meditation means focusing deeply without distraction to cultivate calm. In meditation, we direct our thoughts toward a positive intention, then gently release distractions and return to that focus. Writing about your experience also supports physical and mental growth as you heal.

Let's start the meditation journey together:

Start by taking deep breaths, focusing only on your breathing. Notice the natural rise and fall of your belly. It's okay if your mind wanders. Simply bring your focus back to your breath. Typically, in meditation, you breathe in through your nose and out through your mouth. Keep your eyes closed and continue breathing. You may wish to time yourself: see how long you can maintain focus on your breath. Let this be your intention. A ten-second breath is a solid, mindful breath. Breathe in slowly, filling your diaphragm first, then your lungs, and exhale just as slowly.

> Note: If you'd like to meditate with me, visit https://www.mindshiftwellnesscenter.com/meditation-videos/

Breathing is a fundamental part of our existence; we contribute to the planet's oxygen cycle. We need oxygen to survive! It helps organisms grow, enables our cells to convert food into energy, and even supports reproduction. By learning to focus on our breath, we master a vital life skill. Consider this as you practice the first step of meditation. It's a powerful concept to reflect on periodically throughout your day, bringing mindful intent to your daily breathing. While meditating, strengthen your focus by choosing a mantra and a positive affirmation to guide you.

A mantra is a word, sound, or phrase repeated during meditation to concentrate and calm the mind. It may carry spiritual meaning and can be in any language. A positive affirmation, however, is a concise, empowering statement used to counter negative thoughts, build self-esteem, and foster a positive outlook.

In the following space, write a mantra and affirmation. Your mantra can be like this:

"I create my own path and walk it with joy."

Your affirmation can be like this:

"I believe in and have confidence in myself. I am strong."

Feel free to write down how this felt, to write a mantra and affirmation of what came up for you.

Notes for Chapter 5

Key takeaways

- **Seek a professional therapist to properly work through trauma to process your trauma triggers.**
- **Hurt can be of different kinds, and tangible or intangible hurt can leave a person similarly affected.**
- **Trauma has a sequence of events in our brain machinery. Upon introduction to things that remind you of the traumatic event, your brain fires the same synaptic pattern as it did initially, and you feel the same distress.**
- **The process of healing always begins with acknowledgment.**
- **You will have to learn to accept your mistakes and then forgive yourself as well.**
- **You can recover from your trauma through brain training.**
- **Symbolic rituals or made-up practices, such as role-playing, where you can be the hero you need in the moment, or writing a letter, can help in the steps toward healing.**

Chapter 6: Appreciating Who You Are Today

Have you ever wondered how rarely we appreciate our own existence? More often, we encounter people, even ourselves, grieving and self-blaming, often for things that weren't truly their fault. As we move forward, let's pause to appreciate ourselves. This is the central aim of this chapter.

Self-Appreciation Is Different from Self-Esteem

You may ask how to begin. In a world where widespread kindness can seem idealistic, how do we cultivate gratitude for ourselves? We are taught to appreciate loved ones, possessions, and life's small gifts. But self-appreciation is a distinct practice.

If you struggle to name something you love about yourself, recall a genuine compliment from a friend or acquaintance. Perhaps they said, "I really like how shiny your hair is," or "I admire how efficiently you complete projects." We can be blind to our own strengths, so an outside perspective can help redirect our focus. Self-appreciation starts with gratitude for your physical being. To explore this, let's do a simple exercise.

In the space below, write down at least five things that you love about your body. You can write more if you want, and it can range from the shape, color, trait, or texture of any of your body parts. You can love how your body moves and functions; get creative!

(This may be very difficult for some people. So, I suggest that you don't rush and take your time with this part. Be genuine to yourself, and take it slow.)

____

____

____

____

____

____

____

Appreciating your physical body starts you on a journey of self-love. Now, let's move to our second exercise. Recall that self-appreciation is different from self-esteem. To clarify the difference, let's define self-esteem.

Self-esteem is your personal assessment of self-worth. Unlike the ongoing process of self-appreciation, self-esteem is more a judgment of the respect and admiration you believe you deserve. People with high self-esteem feel worthy of respect, while those with self-doubt or low confidence struggle with low self-esteem.

While the two are often related, remember that self-appreciation is fundamentally about viewing yourself with gratitude and acceptance.

Use the space below to write at least five intangible things about yourself that you like. You can write as many as you like. These can be things from simple habits, your major talents, or a natural ability to do something.

For example: "I appreciate my ability to seek humor in tense situations to de-escalate negative emotions and turn a situation lighter or positive."

____

____

____

____

____

____

____

Science suggests we have a natural tendency to focus on flaws: a negativity bias that can overshadow our strengths. Why do we fixate on shortcomings instead of appreciating ourselves? Often, we internalize critical messages from others or from unrealistic comparisons.

Ms. V. is a high-school English teacher in her late twenties. She came to therapy with a strange problem. She defined it as "a voice in my head that is meaner than anyone has ever been to me out loud."

"I say things to myself that I would never allow a student to say to a classmate," she told me in our first session. "If a kid in my class called another kid worthless, I would intervene immediately. But I call myself worthless dozens of times a day, and I've never once intervened on my own behalf."

We began with awareness. Just noticing, without trying to change anything. Ms. V. kept a simple log for one week, making a mark each time she caught the critic. She came back to the following session pale. "Thirty-seven times in a single day," she said. "That's just what I caught. And most of them were so automatic, so background, that I'd been living inside that noise for years without even hearing it."

Replacing the critic did not happen quickly or cleanly. There were weeks she came in and said it felt pointless. There were weeks she made real progress and then slid back after a difficult day at school. "I thought this would be linear," she said. "I thought if I worked hard enough, it would just stop." It did not stop. It quietened, gradually and unevenly, which is the honest version of the story.

One evening, she sent me a short message between sessions: "Made a mistake on a parent email today. Wrong date. Had to send a correction. First thought: You ruin everything. Second thought: It's the wrong date. You caught it. You fixed it. That's what competent people do." She added, "The second voice was quieter than the first. But it was there."

That second voice was hers. By the end of our work together, she had filled a small notebook with appreciations she wrote each night: "I appreciate my patience with the student who struggles to read aloud."

"I appreciate that I kept showing up this week, even when it was hard."

"I appreciate my ability to find something funny when I need to."

"The critical voice is still there," she told me honestly in our final session. "I don't want to lie to you and say it's gone. But there is another voice now, too, a kinder one. And I'm learning to give that voice more airtime."

This brings us to a key balance: appreciating your abilities is as vital as acknowledging your weaknesses. You can only improve an area you consciously recognize. Let's do a simple exercise to identify some.

In the space below, write down some attributes that you think are your weaknesses.

____

____

____

____

____

____

____

Notice what you feel. This awareness is the first step toward building a stronger version of yourself. Remember, high self-esteem doesn't automatically grant you self-appreciation. Underachievement should not hinder self-appreciation.

Affirm this:

I do not have to achieve anything to appreciate myself.

I do not have to achieve anything to appreciate myself.

I do not have to achieve anything to appreciate myself.

The meaning of success is personal. We attach ideas of success, happiness, and fulfillment to different things, whether through art, science, music, or personal connections. Our diversity is what makes us thrive.

In our digital age, the meaning of success is often narrowed to a few visible milestones. Social media worsens this by encouraging constant comparison with curated highlights of others' lives, a new engagement, or a major promotion. For anyone not meeting those specific benchmarks, this can fuel feelings of inadequacy.

Before comparing, pause and re-evaluate your own metrics. Of course, simply redefining success is easier said than done, particularly in a culture that prioritizes financial achievement. Consider this perspective: In the US, the average life expectancy is roughly 79 years, or about 28,835 days. Most of those days will be spent working, which often means prioritizing career concerns. And when you retire, you will make use of your savings, but wait, you'll look back and see how much time was spent worrying about things that, in hindsight, mattered less than your well-being. While a job is necessary, ask yourself if yours is costing you happiness and growth. Recall canceling dinner with loved ones for a project. How often does overwork keep you from the people and experiences that truly matter? This is the moment to start defining success on your own terms.

Let's understand this with a real-life example.

Mr. N. is a partner at a mid-sized investment firm. He came to therapy during what he described as "the most successful period of my life."

"On paper, everything is exactly where I planned it would be," he said. "The title, the number in my bank account, the apartment, the car. I hit every single metric I set for myself when I was twenty-three. Everyone. So why do I feel like I'm already dead?"

As we worked together over the following months, a pattern emerged. Every milestone he had reached had delivered a brief, bright flare of satisfaction and then nothing. "I made partner, and I felt good for maybe a week," he recalled. "Then my brain immediately recalculated, okay, now you need to be the managing partner. The goal always moves the moment I reach it. I've been running on a treadmill my entire adult life, and I'm exhausted, and I'm nowhere."

The exercise that shifted things was simple: I asked him to write his own definition of success, not the inherited one, not the cultural one, but his. He resisted. "If success isn't the corner office and the number, then what have I been doing?" he said. "What did I sacrifice for?" But he completed it.

What he wrote surprised him. He wanted to be known for depth in his relationships, not the width of his professional network. He wanted time in nature. He wanted to build something with his hands. He wanted to finish the novel he had started and abandoned three times. "None of that fits on a LinkedIn profile," he said, half laughing, half grieving. "You can't quantify 'felt genuinely connected to another human being.'"

He made no dramatic exit from his career. But he started leaving the office at six on Fridays. He called his brother every Sunday, the brother he had not spoken to properly in two years. He joined a woodworking class. He took a full week of annual leave, for the first time in four years, and went hiking in Montana.

"Here is what I've learned," he told me near the end of our work. "The metrics I inherited were other people's metrics. My father's, my firm's, the culture's. They were never actually mine. And chasing someone else's definition of success will hollow you out completely, because even when you reach it, there's nothing there with your name on it." He showed me the definition of success he now kept in his phone: Living in a way I could defend to myself on my deathbed. "That's my metric now," he said. "Everything else is just noise."

Now, it's time for you to write your own definition of success.

In the space below, write down what defines success for you.

Now, write down what you think you are most likely to regret in your old age.

____

____

____

____

____

____

____

Once you have filled the spaces above, pause to reflect. Later, reread your answers. Ask yourself: "Does my definition of success align with my deeper purpose?" Then, compare your two answers: does your current path minimize future regrets? Many elderly individuals report that their biggest regret is time lost to "mindless, self-destructive worry." If they could change one thing, it would be worrying less and living more. They emphasize, "You'll regret the time you never got back."

Do you think you will share that regret?

As we continue exploring self-appreciation, consider the research of Vera Ludwig from the University of Pennsylvania. Ludwig, Brown, and Brewer (2020) identifies two key systems in our brain. One is impulse-driven, led by desires and temptations.[8] The other is our cognitive control system, which uses reason to manage those impulses. Ludwig's work focused on creating harmony between these systems, leading her to develop a practical framework.

This seven-step framework helps people regulate behaviors to align them with their goals and core values. In essence, it bridges the gap between impulsive desires and what you truly want to achieve. For example, if your goal is to read more but you impulsively scroll social media, the first step is recognizing that scrolling is unfulfilling and drains time from your well-being.

Following the steps, you become more aware of your patterns and how changes affect you. Your brain's reward system reinforces positive progress, motivating you to pursue what aligns with your values.

The key lesson is this: align your goals with what genuinely enhances your well-being. This may require redefining what achievement means to you. Now, let's apply these principles of self-appreciation and awareness.

[8] Ludwig, V., Brown, K. W., & Brewer, J. A. (2020). Self-regulation without force. Perspectives on Psychological Science.

Exercise: Take any one of your weaknesses (or several) that you have mentioned previously and write a detailed plan for how you would overcome this particular weakness or change your vision to look at it as if it were a strength.

Good job! I know it wasn't easy, so thank you for engaging deeply with this exercise. As you move forward, examining the many facets of your personality, you'll likely see yourself from a new perspective.

The result may not always be pleasing, and your self-view may not shift dramatically yet. If so, practice patience and trust the process.

Since you've come this far, reward your effort. Treat yourself to something you've wanted, even something small like a favorite coffee. Go to dinner or a movie, choose something you enjoy. You can make this a habit, linking small rewards to your achievements. Most importantly, acknowledge that you deserve it.

By engaging your brain's reward system, you learn to appreciate yourself for small victories, the central message of this chapter. Get comfortable celebrating yourself. You deserve it.

Exercise: *Have fun with this! Write out as much as you can (you can use the space on the next page). Write out everything you appreciate about yourself (internally and externally), your life, the world, and the people around you.*

I will end this chapter with Oprah Winfrey's following words,

"When you undervalue what you do, the world will undervalue who you are."

Notes for Chapter 6

Key Takeaways

- **Self-appreciation is different than self-esteem.**
- **When you attach too much significance to the meaning of success to material things, you will find yourself unhappy and unaccomplished.**
- **A self-reward system can help you in reassessing how you value yourself.**
- **The value of your goals should be examined in a way that promotes your well-being.**

Chapter 7: Principles and Practices

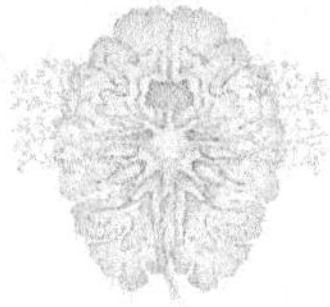

Moving forth in this quest for a fulfilled life through rediscovering ourselves, we now come to the point of discussing some of the streamlined concepts ingrained within psychology. These concepts are backed by scientific data and knowledge and have become the overarching principles, the primary goal of which is self-improvement. The point of this chapter, and by extension, this book, is to introduce and explain these principles and practices so that we can begin a journey of mindfulness on our own. Let's begin with Positive Psychology.

Positive Psychology

While its philosophical roots are ancient, Positive Psychology emerged as a distinct scientific field at the beginning of the 21st century. In that sense, it is a relatively new discipline. What this discipline actually means can be understood with the definition given to us by Peterson (2008):

"Positive Psychology is the scientific study of what makes life most worth living."

In Chapter 2, we discussed the power of optimism. Positive psychology shares this focus, concentrating on building strengths rather than repairing weaknesses.

You might ask, "But isn't fixing weaknesses the path to success?" While addressing flaws has its place, positive psychology proposes that sustained well-being comes more reliably from cultivating what you do best. You don't ignore weaknesses, but you invest your energy where you have the greatest potential for growth and satisfaction.

The core of positive psychology rests on these pillars:

- **Enhancing strength and virtues**
- **Positive events and influences**
- **Positive experiences**
- **Positive states and traits**
- **Positive institutions**

Positive psychology as a distinct field began after Martin Seligman, an American psychologist and educator, realized that psychology as a field should be diverted from the negative influences, such as trauma, mental illnesses, etc., and be used to instill betterment within human behavior. Thus, today, it examines constructive elements like gratitude, happiness, resilience, compassion, and hope.

Respectfully acknowledging the five key figures who played pivotal roles in positive psychology: William James,

Abraham Maslow, Martin Seligman, Mihaly Csikszentmihalyi, Christopher Peterson, Barbara Fredrickson, and Carl Rogers. It is important to acknowledge key contributors to positive psychology, including William James, Abraham Maslow, Martin Seligman, Mihaly Csikszentmihalyi, Christopher Peterson, Barbara Fredrickson, and Carl Rogers.

A central framework within the field is the PERMA model, developed by Seligman.[9]

How it Works:

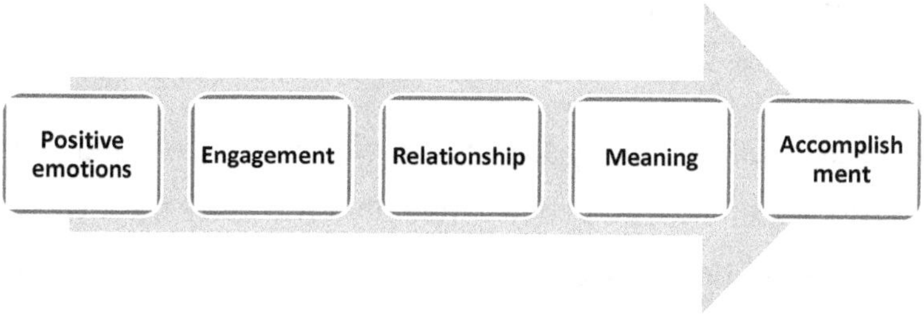

These elements are interconnected and support one another. By focusing on positive emotions, we curate a life based on strong character and well-being, whereas the aspect of engagement lets us pay attention to each task we perform and engage in it with our complete and undivided attention. This way, we will be able to see how this specific aspect contributes to our overall well-being. Relationships that we form within and outside of ourselves have a greater impact on our purposefulness and overall positive outlook on life. Similarly, trying to derive and associate a sense of

[9] Graphics created using Microsoft® Word SmartArt.

meaningfulness in everything that we do also contributes majorly to our positive buildup, and lastly, our sense of well-being flourishes when we shift our focus to trying to accomplish assigned goals. These five overarching aspects of Positive Psychology are dependent upon each other. For example, you decide to switch your job because you can't deal with the negativities of your current work environment. In the prospect of looking for another job, it is important that you avoid repeating the mistakes that previously occurred and ask yourself questions. Consider someone who is unhappy and discontent in their working environment; this can lead to stress.

Positive Psychology studies the effects of stress and how painful experiences can ultimately enrich our lives, known as post-traumatic growth. The field scientifically explores thoughts, feelings, and behaviors that lead to human flourishing, focusing on strengths and positive experiences.

However, Positive Psychology also acknowledges that unpleasant experiences can be crucial in this process. For example, chronic unhappiness is a significant source of stress, which is detrimental to our health and longevity. Painful experiences like loss or unrequited love feed this cycle of stress, which in turn suppresses the positive aspects of the human mind and body.

Given this, isn't it justified to pause and reflect? Even if you're not actively seeking another job, it's worth honestly evaluating your current work environment.

These questions could be:

Does this job contribute to my happiness and satisfaction in my life?

Does this job make me feel like I am living my intended purpose in life?

Does this job contribute to my overall well-being and accomplish my life goals?

____

____

____

____

____

____

List three of the most admirable qualities that you consider to be your strengths:

Strength 1: ____________________________

Strength 2: ____________________________

Strength 3: ____________________________

For each of these strengths, think deeply and answer the following questions. You are allowed to spend no more than 1 hour on this exercise. There's a time crunch here, so note the immediate responses as soon as they appear.

	Strength 1	Strength 2	Strength 3
How do I use this strength already?			

In what areas of my life do I use this strength?			
What other ways could I use this strength?			

Following this exercise, you will be able to see and maximize your potential. For example, if you identified social skills as a strength, the purpose is to discover how to apply this talent in new areas, such as using networking to grow a business or launch a product. Since we are talking about positive influences in life, let me introduce you to existential psychology.

Existentialism

Existentialism, in its simplest definition, is being aware of or inquiring about our existence. It's when we try to make sense of what and who we are, which can often lead to dejection when one feels a lack of purpose.

Existentialism, or existential psychology as a distinct field, reached its peak in mid-20th-century France. Scholars often trace its roots to 19th-century philosophers like Nietzsche and Kierkegaard (though neither used the term). Both philosophers considered the act of making free choices based on fundamental values to be essential to shaping one's identity. But one could argue that existential questioning has existed for as long as humanity itself.

Do not let this potentially complex term scare you off; by the end of this explanation, it will feel deeply relatable.

A lack of purpose can also make people prone to "nihilism," a perspective that life lacks inherent meaning. It's easy to feel lost when you think, 'What is the point of all this struggle?' or 'If we all die, why do we strive so hard?' Sound familiar? Dr. Viktor Frankl, a psychologist, neurologist, philosopher, psychiatrist, and Holocaust survivor, offers a different view. Frankl spent three years in Nazi concentration camps, enduring one of history's most inhumane experiences. He presents his account and his method of "logotherapy" in the book *Man's Search for Meaning* (one of my personal favorites)

The book revolves around the idea that, even in dire circumstances, we can find purpose by focusing on the next meaningful possibility. What does that mean? Before his imprisonment, Frankl was a renowned physician dedicated to his work and theories. When everything was taken from him—his clothes, his manuscript, his status—he still found reasons to strive, even if just for a piece of bread, an extra portion of gravy, or a rare cigarette. In simpler terms, his theory teaches that purpose is woven into daily life; we only need to shift our focus to see it.

Let the wafting fragrance of coffee, the feel of a book, the taste of food, or the laughter of loved ones remind you that these simple pleasures give life meaning and help you endure each day. The pursuit of meaning begins with acknowledging and appreciating yourself, a topic we covered extensively in Chapter 6. Beyond yourself, look around and remind yourself of life's simplest pleasures. In Chapter 1, I introduced the concept of a mindful morning, which can extend into a mindful life. It wouldn't be wrong to say that mindfulness opens the door to meaning and purpose.

The personal mission statement from Chapter 2 also shows how we can align immediate goals with long-term purpose. Now, let's try an assessment based on the work of Barry Schwartz, an American psychologist who studied the paradox of choice.[10] This tool, adapted from positive psychology resources, helps determine whether you tend to be a "maximizer" or a "satisficer."

Write the appropriate number for each answer (with 1 being the least, 7 being the most):

1-2-3-4-5-6-7

---

[10] Schwartz, B., Ward, A., Monterosso, J., Lyubomirsky, S., White, K., & Lehman, D. R. (2002). Maximizing versus satisficing: Happiness is a matter of choice. Journal of Personality and Social Psychology, 83(5), 1178–1197. https://doi.org/10.1037/0022-3514.83.5.1178

	1	2	3	4	5	6	7
I have to channel surf even when I'm already watching a show.	1	2	3	4	5	6	7
I expect a lot from relationships and am always looking for a perfect fit	1	2	3	4	5	6	7
Picking a gift for a friend is very difficult.	1	2	3	4	5	6	7
I can never find clothes I really love	1	2	3	4	5	6	7
When picking a book or article to read, I struggle with picking the best one.	1	2	3	4	5	6	7
I love ratings, and I'm always scanning lists of rankings.	1	2	3	4	5	6	7
Even when I send a simple email, I always do several drafts.	1	2	3	4	5	6	7

I hold myself to the highest standards in everything I do.	1	2	3	4	5	6	7
I always tell people to never settle for the second-best.	1	2	3	4	5	6	7
I always fantasize about having another better life	1	2	3	4	5	6	7

Add up all your scores and write it down here: ______

If your score is 40 or less, you are a satisficer, which means that you are generally satisfied with your life and have the ability to fight dissatisfaction.

If your score is 65 or more, you are more likely to be a maximizer, and you may find it a little challenging to indulge in behaviors that contribute to your overall well-being. However, don't be dejected, as this can signify the beginning of your journey.

What are positive inquiry questions? Succinctly put, an appreciative or positive question is "a question that seeks to uncover and bring out the best in a person, a situation, or an organization." (Whitney et al., 2002: 89)

Positive inquiry questions are questions designed to focus on the strengths, successes, and positive aspects of a person, situation, or organization.

Instead of dwelling on problems or shortcomings, these questions aim to uncover and highlight the best qualities, achievements, and growth potential. They encourage reflection, optimism, and a constructive approach to understanding and improving circumstances.

Exercise: Here's a short exercise to practice this:

1. Identify a Topic: Choose a topic or area of focus that you want to explore using positive inquiry. It could be about personal goals, a recent achievement, a work project, or any other aspect of your life.

2. Generate Positive Inquiry Questions: Brainstorm a list of questions that focus on the positive aspects of your chosen topic. Here are some examples:

- What strengths did I demonstrate in achieving this goal?

____

____

____

____

____

____

____

- What aspects of this project have been most successful?

____

____

____

____

____

____

- How have I grown personally or professionally through this experience?

____

____

- What resources or support have helped me along the way?

- What lessons have I learned that I can apply to future endeavors?

3. Reflect and Respond: Take some time to reflect on each question and jot down your responses. Focus on the strengths, achievements, and positive outcomes associated with your topic.

4. Share and Discuss: If possible, share your reflections with a trusted friend, colleague, or mentor. Discuss your insights, discoveries, and any actionable steps you can take based on your reflections.

5. Repeat and Refine: Make positive inquiry a regular practice by incorporating it into your daily or weekly routine. Continuously refine your questions and reflections to deepen your understanding and appreciation of the positives in your life.

____

____

____

____

____

____

____

By engaging in this exercise, you'll develop a habit of focusing on the positive aspects of your experiences and fostering a mindset of growth and possibility.

Good work!! Now let's move on to our next step!!

Rewriting Our Narrative in Our Life

Consider the possibility of rewriting your story completely. So, instead of "Nelly suffered a traumatic episode and struggled to form stable relationships," the story could become, "Nelly learned immensely from that incident and promised herself never to repeat those mistakes."

I understand that healing from trauma is far more complex than a simple shift in perspective. Yet, as I've emphasized throughout this book, a changed perspective is often the crucial first step. I often explain this to my patients with a metaphor.

Without judging my drawing skills, consider the diagram on the left. It shows you as the observer of an event from a single, fixed point.

This represents a unidirectional view. Now, imagine the event at the center of a circle. Every point on the circumference offers a different angle to view it, each revealing a distinct part of the picture.

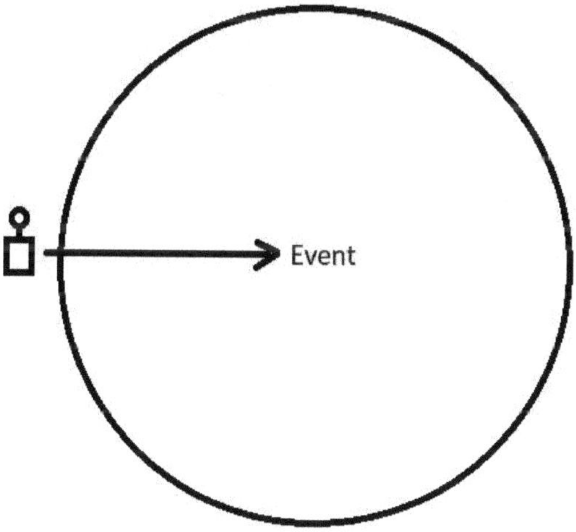

A circle contains 360 degrees, and an infinite number of viewpoints exist between them. The point is to learn to show yourself alternative perspectives. Sometimes, all we need is to step away from the one angle we've been fixed on.

That explains *how* to see events from new angles, but how do we actually rewrite the narrative?

Let's understand with an example.

One of my clients was Ms. G. She was a forty-five-year-old woman who had grown up in chronic poverty and built a stable life. The reason for her coming to therapy was that, despite genuine accomplishments, she could not stop telling herself the story of someone who was perpetually on the verge of losing everything.

"I own my home," she said in our second session. "I have savings. I have a good job I've held for nine years. My children are healthy and doing well in school. By every measure, I am safe. And yet I wake up every single morning convinced today is the day it all falls apart." She pressed her hands together. "The anxiety is exhausting. I can't enjoy anything because I'm always waiting for it to be taken away. My husband says I live like we're still poor, even though we're not. He's right. I don't know how to live any other way."

As we explored her history, the narrative became clear. She had grown up in a household where financial struggles were the norm. The story she had constructed to survive that environment had helped her build the stable life she now had. But the story had not updated. She was still operating from the old script in a changed setting.

"Your narrative kept you safe," I told her. "It was true for a long time. The question is whether it's still true now and whether it's costing you more than it's protecting you." She sat with that. "It costs me everything," she said quietly. "I can't enjoy my own life. I have everything I ever worked for, and I can't be in it."

We worked on writing a counter-narrative, not a denial of her history, but an update. The old story: *I am someone who loses things and must always be braced for the next loss.*

The new story: *I am someone who survived real hardship and built real safety, and I am allowed to inhabit that safety now.*

"It felt dishonest at first," she admitted. But she practiced it by reading the new narrative aloud each morning, inserting evidence from her actual life to support it. The home she owned. The nine years of stability. The savings account she could verify was still there.

In one of our final sessions, she told me, "I don't think the vigilance ever will be entirely gone. It's been there too long. But it has quietened. Some mornings I wake up, and the first thought isn't 'what's about to go wrong.' Sometimes the first thought is just... I'm here. This is mine. I built this. Do you know how long I've waited to be able to think that? To actually believe it?"

Have you experienced a situation like my client, Ms. G? If yes, this exercise will help you break free from the worries keeping you from seeing the bright side of the picture.

In the space below, identify three specific issues that, if you resolved them now, would significantly change your life. Describe each in one clear sentence.

For example: If only I had more money, I could pay all my debts and start the business that I have been meaning to start for a very long time; that won't happen. OR I'll never get a raise because they don't value me.

1:____

____

____

____

2:____

____

____

____

3:____

____

____

____

I want you to read and reread what you have written before continuing from here. This previous exercise is a demonstration of what story you keep telling yourself. If you have written here things that relate to the acquisition of more money, capital, time, or something relating to how you have or had a misfortune of luck or circumstances, you will need to change your story.

The narrative that we keep telling ourselves contributes the most to how we approach our final goals in life. In an experiment conducted on people with somewhat narcissistic tendencies, it was found that their self-esteem had grown manifold after a positive self-affirmation exercise was introduced into their routines. Now, it is not necessary for you to have similar tendencies, but we will take away the important lesson from here, which is to ingrain habits such as self-affirmations (you can revisit the end of Chapter 5 for our affirmation exercises).

Now, taking the example where the subject assumed that having more money could resolve all their problems, let us see how a change of narrative can be approached. So, instead of:

"If only I had more money, I could pay all my debts and start the business that I have been meaning to start for a very long time; that won't happen."

It could be:

My rising debts mean I have not been careful enough with my money. I need to have a strategy and look after my expenditure habits; maybe this way, I can finally have the money I need to establish the business I have so long dreamt of. And "I'll never get a raise because they don't value me" to "I am a valuable employee. I will look for more ways to make myself invaluable, and I'll ask for a raise because I am worth it; if I don't get it this time, it's okay; I'll get it eventually."

In the same way, let's provide counterarguments to the three statements written above the exercise—one for each—to offer a broader and more balanced perspective.

Counter 1:

____

____

____

____

Counter 2:

____

____

____

____

Counter 3:

____

____

____

____

Good job

Now, to conclude this chapter, we have learned that while it is easy to fall into the pits of sadness and dejection, and tempting to shut off from the world, this can be countered through simpler concepts. We can focus on and build our strengths, as taught by Positive Psychology, and discover purposefulness in the smaller activities of our day. Furthermore, the root of our despondency or lack of meaning often lies in the personal narrative we tell ourselves. Changing this internal story is essential work for building a more fulfilled life.

Notes for Chapter 7

Key Takeaways:

- **Positive psychology revolves around the idea of strengthening your self-esteem by focusing on your strengths and making use of your weaknesses.**
- **You can use your various strengths in more ways than you think is possible.**
- **Adding meaning to your life does not need a higher purpose; it can be achieved through the simplest pleasures of life.**
- **The story that you tell or the narrative that you paint affects your entire well-being, including your future prospects.**
- **Sometimes, all you need is a change of all angles from which you view an event. Pick a healthier perspective.**

Chapter 8: A Nourishing Relationship with Yourself

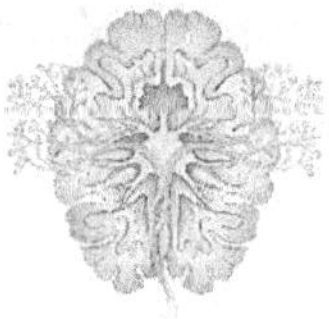

"I'd rather be hated for who I am than loved for who I am not."

-Kurt Cobain

Relationships form the bedrock of our lives, shaping our experiences with partners, family, and friends. These connections do more than fill our days; they have a profound influence on how we see ourselves. Yet this dynamic is paradoxical, for our self-image, in turn, colors every personal bond we form.

To understand how others help shape our identity, we can look to psychology. Freudian theory, for instance, explores how childhood experiences solidify into adult beliefs. A trauma inherited from a loved one at a young age can distort one's view of love, which is why those raised in abusive households often show a deep reluctance to form stable, long-term attachments.

This raises a critical question: Does a childhood deprived of healthy affection or marked by trauma condemn one to a lifetime of unstable relationships? It does not.

We are blessed with what scientists call plastic brains. This is not a literal description but a metaphor for neuroplasticity, the brain's remarkable ability to reshape itself. A wealth of literature confirms that the abusive and unhealthy patterns carved into our past are not permanent. Through deliberate practice, these neural pathways can be remolded, offering a path forward beyond the shadows of earlier years.

What does this mean?

Simply put, the mirage you believe in, the distorted reflection of yourself, sets the tone for every interaction and bond you form. While a hundred reasons may lie behind low self-esteem, clinging to a tarnished self-image can manifest as a complaining partner, a distant child, or an absent friend. This dynamic is captured succinctly by Robert Holden: "The relationship with yourself sets the tone for every other relationship you have."

Often, the struggle to maintain our bonds stems primarily from the story we repeat to ourselves. If a false personal narrative is the core of the issue, the exercise in Chapter 7 can guide you in reframing that story positively. But suppose the problem feels deeper than narrative. Research confirms that low self-esteem directly warps how you believe your partner perceives you. Many of us fixate on a perceived physical flaw, one our partner may never have noticed, yet it looms large in our own mind. This persistent insecurity and self-criticism can, over time, subtly alter a partner's actual perception, creating a self-fulfilling prophecy. Given the choice, is not the confident individual, who embraces their whole self, inherently more inviting than one ashamed of their own existence?

Imagine being with someone too fearful to learn the art of self-love. Initially, compassion or affection might compel you to become their pillar, constantly reassuring them of their worth.

While such devotion is not always a reason to part, it often leads onto rocky terrain, where one person is exhausted by the cyclical burden of propping up the other's fragile self-image. Therefore, the path out of the insecurities that damage our relationships begins with self-love. The essential question follows: how do we cultivate it? The journey requires deliberate practice. We begin by:

Discarding Opinions and Comparisons

As social animals, we cannot claim total immunity from the opinions of others. The deeper problem, however, lies in the significance we grant them, and more than half of this weight comes from opinions that exist only in our own minds. When we perceive someone as better, it aggravates our fragile self-image, triggering a mental inventory of their superior body, face, wealth, or status.

A powerful mental exercise is to visualize discarding these thoughts. Create an imaginary receptacle in your mind. The moment you feel diminished by comparison, or when you cling too tightly to another's judgment, consciously place that thought inside it and let it go. The deliberate act of visualization makes the process tangible, transforming a passive worry into an active release. From there, we must move to a more courageous practice:

Facing Your Fears

True self-love is built upon a foundation of self-acceptance, which begins when you confront your fears directly. Ask yourself: what are you truly afraid of? What would happen if you stepped out without covering a perceived flaw? What if you learned to say no?

Growth is impossible without facing and dismantling these fears, be they of rejection, judgment, or failure. As explored earlier, we remain stunted until we move through them. For those whose fears feel overwhelming, seeking professional guidance is a profound act of courage. A psychoanalyst or an EMDR therapist can provide essential pathways to healing, while modalities like biofeedback or hypnotherapy may offer valuable supplementary support.

The final, crucial step is to audit your environment. Insecurities are not always internally generated; they can be fueled from the outside. The link between self-esteem and relationships is reciprocal; each continuously affects the other. Therefore, as you work on self-acceptance, you must also ask, "Am I surrounded by toxic influences?" You may instinctively answer "no," for toxicity is often subtle and normalized. To identify it, you must look closer. Consider these questions:

Is your friend/partner constantly complaining about everything?

____

____

Do they always judge people in their lives?

____

____

Do they make you feel like you're not enough?

____

____

Is their behavior passive-aggressive with you?

____

____

Do you not feel like being yourself around them?

____

____

If you find this person toxic, it's time to evaluate. Clear the clutter! Stay true to yourself and make room for positive people/outside sources who let you shine bright!

Let's understand this with an example.

One of my clients, Ms. W., was a twenty-nine-year-old nurse. She came to therapy because she always felt exhausted and did not know why. Her sleep was adequate. Her physical health was good. Her job, demanding as it was, was one she found genuinely meaningful. She had, by her own account, no obvious reason to feel so drained.

It took several sessions before her closest friendship came up. She described her friend of twelve years with a mixture of loyalty and something she kept trying not to call resentment. "She's been through a lot," Ms. W. said carefully. "I don't want to be unsympathetic."

I asked her to tell me about a typical interaction.

She described phone calls that lasted ninety minutes and left her feeling flattened. There was a pattern where Ms. W.'s problems were described as "not that bad" while her friend's equivalent difficulties were treated as catastrophic. "But she's been through a lot," Ms. W. said again, as if reminding herself.

"Has she been through more than you?" I asked.

Long silence. "No," she said finally. "Honestly, no. But somehow her pain always takes up more room than mine. My problems don't seem to count as much." Another pause. "I don't actually feel like I can be myself around her. I edit what I say. I manage her reactions before I open my mouth." She looked at me. "That's not a friendship, is it?"

It was not a question.

The work that followed was not about ending the friendship immediately or dramatically. It was about helping Ms. W. see clearly what had been normalized over twelve years until it had come to feel like what friendship simply was. "I thought loving someone meant making yourself smaller so they had more room," she said in one session. "I didn't realize I'd been shrinking for a decade."

She eventually reduced contact significantly, a decision that came with genuine grief alongside the relief. "I miss who I thought she was," Ms. W. said. "I think I've been grieving that person for a while, actually. The friendship I thought I had." She straightened slightly. "But I've stopped being exhausted for no reason. Turns out there was a reason. There's always a reason."

This example teaches how easily emotional depletion can be mistaken for something internal, when in reality it is often shaped by the dynamics we tolerate around us. Setting boundaries is not an act of rejection, but one of self-respect. It requires recognizing where your energy is being diminished and allowing yourself the space to restore balance. This does not always mean cutting people off abruptly, but rather becoming more intentional and observing what a relationship gives as well as what it takes. When there is a persistent imbalance, creating distance or redefining limits becomes not only reasonable but necessary.

You're Only Human. A crucial part of this path is embracing your own humanity, learning to forgive your mistakes, and accepting that imperfection is not a failure but a condition of being alive. When life brings inconvenience or error, meet it with the reminder that you are only human. Growth springs not from flawless performance, but from the lessons learned through missteps and the compassion we extend to ourselves and others in their wake. Your Worth Doesn't Lie in Your Looks. This compassion must extend to your physical self. To dismantle the mirage, you must actively reject the distorted standards amplified by social media and entertainment, which preach that your worth is housed in your appearance. Equating your identity solely to physical attributes is a direct recipe for self-loathing. Your fundamental worth is rooted in your existence itself. Each breath is an affirmation that you are here, a living participant in a world of possibility.

Look in the mirror. What do you see? Go beyond the "physical attributes" and look deep into your eyes. If you notice five negative things, then counter that with five positive things. Dwell there until you find them. Note the shift in feeling that occurs when you challenge the automatic negative narrative.

____

____

____

All of this work culminates in a final, essential practice:

Celebrate Yourself

Whoever you are and whatever accomplishments you have at this moment, you have the right to celebrate yourself. Give yourself a break and treat yourself to something you love or have wanted to do. For until you grasp that your own existence is fundamentally essential, you cannot truly learn to cherish the person you see in the mirror.

In the space below, write down at least five things you have wanted to do for yourself.

Tell us about your idea of fun. What activities do you engage in to achieve that feeling?

____

____

____

____

____

____

Remember: The longer you take to cherish yourself and honor the feelings inside you, the longer you will recognize your actual worth. Only you can do that!

Cognitive Behavioral Therapy (CBT)

Cognitive Behavioral Therapy, a cornerstone of modern psychological practice, offers a practical framework for the work of reshaping your mirage. Developed in the 1960s by Professor Aaron Beck at the University of Pennsylvania, CBT has become a mainstream psychotherapeutic treatment for a range of conditions, from anxiety to depression.

While it is strongly recommended to undertake CBT with a licensed therapist, particularly for serious emotional difficulties, its core principles can be applied independently to cultivate greater self-awareness.

The power of CBT lies in a fundamental insight: our minds often operate on automatic, habitual thought patterns, many of which are negatively skewed.

We routinely indulge in distortions and catastrophic thinking that originate from these patterns, which actively hinder our growth and peace. CBT provides the tools to first identify these automatic negative thoughts, then to consciously challenge and alter them, replacing distortions with more balanced and realistic perspectives.

What Is Cognitive Behavioral Therapy (CBT)?

At its core, CBT is a psycho-social intervention aimed at transforming the unhelpful cognitive patterns that dictate our emotions and behaviors. To utilize it, understanding its key premises is essential.

First, our thoughts directly inform our actions. Many of these thoughts are ingrained during moments of past emotional intensity, leaving our minds to run on an autopilot mode prone to self-victimization, diminished self-worth, and fear.

Second, with repetition, these thought patterns strengthen through our lived experiences, eventually solidifying into a perceived reality.

Finally, the work of CBT involves learning to encounter these entrenched patterns. This process reveals how our foundational view of ourselves and life is often rooted in past unpleasant moments. By courageously facing these moments, challenging the automatic thoughts they trigger, and developing rational, balanced explanations, we can begin to undo the damage.

Consider this example. Leah chose an expensive dress for her 30th birthday, wanting the night to be perfect. Frank, her boyfriend of five months, texted to say he would arrive directly from an unavoidable work meeting. Leah's face fell. *Why can't he put me first, just once?* she thought. At the restaurant, her sandstone midi dress drew admiring glances, but Frank was nowhere to be seen. Her disappointment curdled into fixation: *He's so neglectful, even today.*

When Frank arrived twenty minutes late, bearing a bouquet of her favorite flowers, Leah barely acknowledged the gesture. The night ended in a bitter fight, and they returned to their separate apartments, a relationship shattered.

Many would sympathize with Leah, casting Frank as the villain. CBT, however, shifts the focus from the event itself to our interpretation of it. Perhaps Frank's job security depended on that meeting. Perhaps he was late because he rushed to change, not wanting to appear as a tired salesman on her special day. The practice involves moving beyond initial emotion to examine the facts rationally.

In Leah's case, her high expectations and immediate descent into a negative narrative, "He is neglectful," created a self-fulfilling prophecy. This illustrates the autopilot mind in action: a single triggering event (his lateness) activated a deep-seated thought pattern ("I am not a priority"), which dictated a damaging behavior (withholding gratitude, inciting a fight), ultimately confirming her own fearful belief.

Many recognize themselves in Leah's reaction—the swift, internal leap to a conclusion that fuels self-doubt and distress. Cognitive Behavioral Therapy provides a structured method to intercept that leap, to examine each triggering event with realism before it solidifies into a negative belief.

Whether the goal is the reformation of a relationship, the restoration of self-belief, or the rejuvenation of one's capacity for joy, CBT offers a practical framework for profound change.

Foundational tips for this work have been woven throughout these chapters. Among them, the practice of journaling, specifically maintaining a gratitude journal, holds particular power. While a separate journal is useful for the exercises in this book, a dedicated gratitude journal serves a distinct purpose: it actively trains your focus toward meaning and appreciation, anchoring you closer to what is truly worthwhile.

Beyond journaling, which illuminates your thought patterns, you can apply a simple, repeatable exercise whenever faced with an adverse situation.

When anxiety or distress arises from a negative event, pause and work through these steps: Think of the recent adverse incident. As a CBT practice, structure your reflection by filling in the following information. (Beck, 2020)[11]

Situation
Describe the situation that triggered your negative thinking
Negative Thoughts
What went through your mind? (thoughts, images, or memories)
Emotions and Body Feelings
What did you feel? Where in your body did you feel it? How strong was this feeling on a distress level? (0-10)

[11] Beck, J. S. (2020). Cognitive behavior therapy: Basics and beyond (3rd ed.). Guilford Press.

Responses
What did you do? How did you cope with those feelings?
What should you have done differently? How could you have changed your response?

You can use this table for monitoring your self-criticism or if your habits get too self-destructive. What you have to do is simply replace the section of "Negative Thoughts" with "Self-critical Thoughts" or just "Thoughts." Ask yourself questions such as;

Feel free to answer these questions in correspondence to the above exercise.

What were you predicting would happen?

What did it mean to you?

As you diligently document these inconvenient episodes, you will begin to notice a subtle but powerful shift in your thought patterns. This practice trains the mind to observe events not as personal catastrophes but as situations open to interpretation, fostering a more balanced and resilient 1q perspective. This transformation requires consistent work, but the trajectory it sets is toward fundamental change.

CBT provides a proven framework for this renewal. By learning to build a more robust and healthy relationship with yourself through its principles, you naturally create the foundation for more beneficial and stable connections with partners, friends, and family.

To further this work, the next step is increased self-identification. Begin by reviewing the following list of common cognitive distortions, noting which patterns you recognize most in your own thinking.

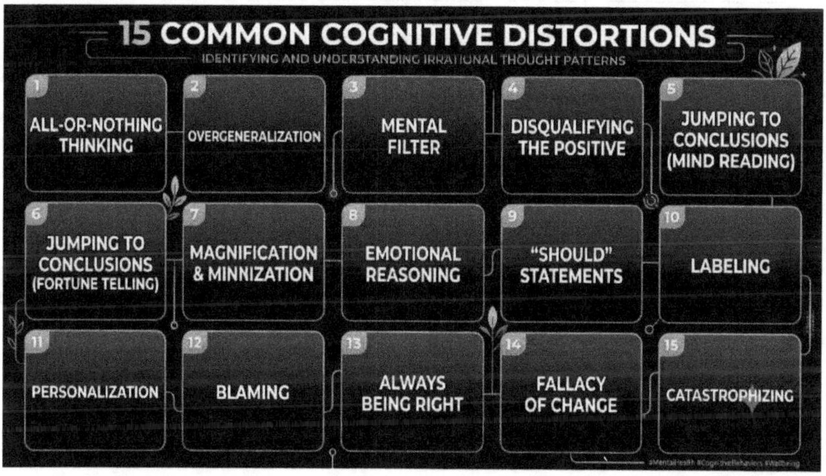

Identifying your characteristic cognitive distortions is the critical first step.

The ongoing work lies in consciously diminishing their power by replacing them with healthier, more accurate thoughts. This process of cognitive replacement is where profound personal transformation takes root.

For distortions that feel deeply entrenched, partnering with a licensed therapist can provide the necessary guidance for a meaningful deep dive.

Whether undertaken independently or with professional support, the fundamental method remains the same: you must interrogate the distortion.

Begin by asking yourself:

Notes for Chapter 8

Key Takeaways

- **Forming healthier relationships with others begins by forming healthy relationships with yourself.**
- **Self-love begins with discarding judgments and accepting yourself as who you are.**
- **People cannot respect you unless you respect yourself.**
- **You are worth more than your physical appearance.**
- **CBT can help you undo the toxic and negative thought patterns.**
- **Begin by asking yourself if your worries are stemming from self-insufficiency.**
- **Let CBT help you with self-loathing, self-criticism, and negative thoughts.**
- **For every negative thought or comment, replace it with five positive ones.**
- **Neuroplasticity: You can change your brain.**

Chapter 9: Am I a Sensitive Person?

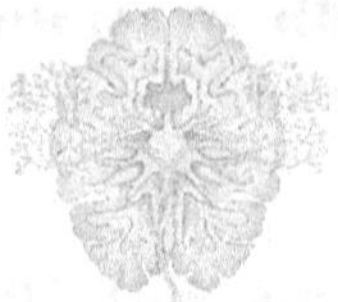

Sensitivity describes the intensity of one's reaction to the environment, both physical and emotional. A person might be sensitive to cold, to discomfort, or to an allergen. This reactive capacity extends profoundly to the emotional realm. To be emotionally sensitive is to be highly attuned, to possess a deep compassion, a considerate nature, and a sharp capability to detect the feelings of others. It involves an acute consciousness of their needs and a desire to act in ways that provide comfort.

This trait offers significant benefits. It sharpens our response to surroundings and people, heightens awareness of potential threats, and forms the very foundation of empathy. Sensitivity aids in building and sustaining both professional and personal connections, and it informs more thoughtful decision-making. Introducing a difficult new rule at work, for example, requires the sensitive forethought to consider its impact and anticipate reactions.

Yet, when sensitivity becomes excessive, it carries downsides, affecting relationships, work, and psychological health. This duality explains the trait's complex reputation. If the ability to be vulnerable and deeply attuned is a strength, why does "sensitive" so often bear a negative connotation?

Highly Sensitive People (HSP)

Individuals with a heightened sensitivity are often mislabeled as "high-strung." A Highly Sensitive Person (HSP) experiences stronger, more intense reactions to sensory, emotional, and social stimuli: a trait sometimes referred to as Sensory Processing Sensitivity. This is not a disorder but an innate characteristic, believed to affect roughly twenty percent of the population, with its own unique set of challenges and strengths.

The experience of an HSP is dual-natured. Their profound attunement can lead them to overreact to benign, playful interactions or everyday stresses. Yet this same sensitivity grants them an almost intuitive ability to comprehend underlying tensions or bad intentions, even in situations where they are not directly involved. They sense the emotional climate more quickly and are often more deeply impacted by negative events.

Their assets—deep kindness, a loving nature, and a powerful capacity for empathy—make them incredibly appealing and devoted friends. Paradoxically, these very qualities can leave them vulnerable to being exploited, which in turn reinforces their guardedness.

This reminds me of the story of a client of mine, Ms. N, who experienced this. She was a fifty-two-year-old librarian who came to therapy describing herself as "broken in a way I can't explain to people who aren't like this." She had spent years trying to find language for her experience and consistently failed to make others understand.

In our first session, she told me how everyone always thought she was overreacting and how it had been affecting her life. "I get so affected by everything that everyone thinks I'm overreacting. If a friend cancels plans at the last minute, I'm devastated for days. Someone raises their voice slightly in a meeting, and my heart races for hours afterward. I walk into a crowded restaurant, and I'm overwhelmed before I've even sat down. I sometimes feel like I have some emotional antenna that keeps picking up everyone's stress. I wish I could just switch it off."

Upon further discussions, we discovered that she was always known as too emotional, too reactive, and too sensitive since childhood.

"For years, I tried to be less affected by things. It never worked. I just got better at hiding it and worse at handling it."

What Ms. N. considered an overreaction was actually Sensory Processing Sensitivity, which is commonly known as being a Highly Sensitive Person. Her reactions seemed over the top because her nervous system was genuinely processing stimuli more deeply than most people's.

Besides feeling the difficult things more intensely, she also felt beauty, connection, and music more intensely.

"Our culture doesn't have room for that kind of responsiveness," she said. "It only has room for people who can brush things off."

Together, we worked on helping make her sensitivity more manageable. Over time, she learned what she needed to regulate her emotions, for instance, recovery time after social events, build in buffer periods between stimulating activities, and stop apologizing for needing what she needed.

Now, she no longer tries to convince people that her reactions are legitimate. "I know they are, and that's enough," she told me months into our work. "My nervous system is built differently, and I'm learning to work with that reality instead of fighting it as if it's a moral failure."

This might raise an important question in someone who is highly sensitive:

Is it possible to manage high sensitivity?

The straightforward answer is yes.

Navigating this high sensitivity requires conscious strategy. Because HSPs are so emotionally attuned, even minor events can have a significant impact. The following practices can help in managing this intense receptivity:

- ***Knowing Your Triggers:*** **Self-knowledge is paramount. A complete understanding of your** specific vulnerabilities allows you to anticipate and, when possible, avoid scenarios that cause disproportionate disturbance.

- ***The Practice of Meditation:*** Mindfulness and meditation are powerful tools for calming the intrusive thoughts and emotional static that brew within. Balance your routine by consciously planning your day to include both stimulating activities and dedicated periods for quiet restoration.
- ***Creating Relaxing Zones:*** Designate a space in your home as a sanctuary: a corner for listening to soothing music, reading, or simply being without distraction. This becomes a physical refuge where you can channel a more positive, grounded state.
- ***Prioritizing Self-Care:*** The toll of high sensitivity on mental and physical health is real. Developing personal coping mechanisms is essential to avoid over-reliance on others. Exploring gentle, somatic practices like Tai Chi or Reiki can offer pathways to restore internal balance and align scattered emotional energy.
- ***Establishing Healthy Boundaries:*** This is the most critical practice. Clear boundaries must be established, not only in intimate relationships but also with the wider world. This requires you to know what you value and what you will tolerate.

From that clarity comes the strength to communicate your limits, create necessary distance, or walk away from draining situations: an act of kindness to yourself that is anything but unkind.

Empaths

An empath possesses a profound sensitivity to the emotions and energies of others. This capacity extends beyond the keen perception of a Highly Sensitive Person; an empath does not merely comprehend what others feel but can intuitively absorb and experience those feelings as if they were their own, operating on a deeply emotional and often physical level. While all empaths are highly sensitive, not all highly sensitive people experience this level of absorptive empathy.

Neurology offers a potential clue to this trait in the form of "mirror neurons," brain cells that activate both when we perform an action and when we observe someone else performing it. These neurons are thought to be the foundation for empathy, action understanding, and learning through imitation. Current understanding suggests that the density and activity of these neural systems may vary from person to person, which could explain the pronounced empathetic capacity of an empath.

Experience confirms this spectrum. We have all met people exceptionally gifted at gauging our emotions and others seemingly detached from the feelings of anyone around them.

This places empathy on a scale, ranging from the acutely attuned to the clinically devoid (as in psychopathy). This raises two personal questions: where do you fall on that scale, and at what point does high empathy define you as an empath?

To explore this, begin by observing the depth of your connection to others and the intensity of your emotional and physical reactions to charged situations. Here is a popular self-assessment quiz developed by Dr. Judith Orloff, a psychiatrist and author of The Empath's Survival Guide: Life Strategies for Sensitive People.[12] If you find yourself answering "yes" to most of the following questions, you may possess an empath's nature:

Do you ever find yourself absorbing the stress of others?

[Yes] [No]

Have you ever been chastised for being overly sensitive?

[Yes] [No]

Do crowded places make you feel overstimulated?

[12] Orloff, J. (n.d.). Are you an empath? 20 question self-assessment test. Dr. Judith Orloff. https://drjudithorloff.com/quizzes/are-you-an-empath-20-question-self-assessment-test/

[Yes] [No]

Do others think you're empathetic?

[Yes] [No]

Do you feel like being a misfit?

[Yes] [No]

Have you ever felt overreacting to petty issues?

[Yes] [No]

Do you feel drained when exposed to intense emotions?

[Yes] [No]

Do you often feel like you need to fit in?

[Yes] [No]

Do you overeat to cope with stress?

[Yes] [No]

Do you startle easily?

[Yes] [No]

Do you react strongly to caffeine or medications?

[Yes] [No]

Do you have chemical sensitivities or can't tolerate scratchy clothes?

[Yes] [No]

Do you avoid emotionally impactful media?

[Yes] [No]

Do you naturally be the person everyone confides in?

[Yes] [No]

Various frameworks exist to help identify empathic traits. Some specialists focus on the social experience, questioning if you often feel you don't fit in. Others highlight sensory and emotional overwhelm, such as finding the news unbearable or depressing films overpowering.

In the absence of clinical diagnostics, identifying as an empath involves a degree of self-recognition, a deep, personal resonance with the trait's core experience of absorptive empathy.

The Advantages of Being an Empath

This profound attunement carries significant strengths. By intuitively delving into the emotions of those around you, you can more easily comprehend and provide for the people who matter most. Recognizing hidden sadness, loneliness, or fear in others places you in a unique position to offer support, thereby earning deep trust and becoming a person others rely on. This capacity can foster richer, more intimate friendships and partnerships.

Furthermore, this deep intuition often serves as a powerful internal guide. An empath's sensitivity to underlying energies makes them difficult to deliberately deceive or manipulate. If they find themselves mistreated, it is typically because they overrode their initial, accurate instincts about a person, not because they failed to sense the warning indicators.

Disadvantages of Being an Empath:

Of course, this profound emotional attachment carries serious drawbacks. Research suggests empaths are quickly overwhelmed in crowded places or at intensely emotional gatherings like weddings or funerals, as they unconsciously absorb the collective mood around them. This can rapidly become exhausting and depleting. Empaths may find it difficult to relax, their inner state constantly colored by the feelings of others. Without a method to process this continuous influx of external stimuli, they can struggle with sleep and the maintenance of their psychological health. Furthermore, not everyone welcomes such acute perception. Despite helpful intentions, your insights into another's hidden moods can sometimes be perceived as intrusive or unnerving, creating unexpected social friction.

The most critical skill for an empath or highly sensitive person is discernment: the ability to distinguish which emotions in your sphere are authentically yours, and which have been absorbed from others. For instance, a sudden wave of agitation may not be your own. Did it arise after a specific person entered your space? Does their energy seem aggressive? If so, the feeling likely belongs to them. Cultivating this moment-to-moment awareness is the first step toward establishing necessary emotional boundaries.

The Strength of Vulnerability

"Vulnerability is the core, the heart, and the center of meaningful human experiences."

-Brené Brown

Several deep misconceptions surround vulnerability, which is persistently linked with fear, shame, and weakness. It is seen as the handmaiden to rejection and failure, a state to be avoided at all costs. This lesson is profoundly ingrained, particularly in young boys, fostering a culture where emotional suppression is mistaken for strength. As a result, we learn to evade vulnerability instinctively, failing to recognize that this very openness, though branded a weakness, is in fact a vital and non-negotiable part of a full human experience.

Many clients come to me with the same issue. One of them was Ms. D., a forty-eight-year-old attorney. She had built a successful career on projecting absolute competence and control. What led her to therapy was, in her own words, "a humiliating public breakdown that should never have happened to someone like me."

In our first session, she appeared completely emotionally shattered. She then described how a routine hearing had escalated unexpectedly, leading to a judge making some criticism, and suddenly she was crying in open court.

I could see the embarrassment on her face as she described what had happened.

"I had to excuse myself. Everyone saw. My colleagues, my opponents, the clerk. I cried in front of everyone, and I couldn't stop."

I realized that what she had framed as catastrophic failure was, in fact, her nervous system finally refusing to keep on the mask she'd been wearing for twenty-five years. The breakdown was the collapse of an unsustainable performance of invulnerability. Upon detailed discussion, we discovered that the issue started way back in her childhood, when her father did not care much about emotional expression. For instance, he'd leave the room when she cried. This gave her the message that her feelings were unacceptable. So, she learned to suppress them.

However, the cost of that suppression had been compounding silently for decades. It led to failed relationships because she couldn't let anyone truly see her, stress-related health problems, and a pervasive sense of isolation despite being surrounded by colleagues and acquaintances.

"I was successful and completely alone," she explained. "I'd never let anyone close enough to see that I was human."

We worked slowly on what vulnerability actually meant. It took some time to convince her that her vulnerability was just the conscious choice to be seen honestly. This terrified her in ways that cross-examination never had.

Eventually, she tried opening up and talked about her struggles with her close friend. To her surprise, she received a positive response.

"My friend said, 'I know. I've been waiting for you to tell me.' She'd known the entire time. My perfect performance had fooled no one."

Slowly, tentatively, she began experimenting with measured vulnerability in safe relationships. Admitting when she didn't know something. Asking for help. Expressing genuine emotion instead of the carefully curated version. "Every single time, I expected rejection or judgment. And every single time, the opposite happened. People got closer, not farther away."

Six months into our work, she returned to court for the first time since the breakdown and handled a difficult opposing counsel with a composure that was qualitatively different from her old control.

Her whole life, Ms. D. was taught that vulnerability was the opposite of strength. That it would destroy her credibility, career, and her worth, until she learned that it's actually the foundation of strength.

Yet understanding this truth intellectually is very different from confronting it in real life, where the fear of being seen often feels far more powerful than the need to be authentic.

The exercise below will help you first identify and then confront the fear of vulnerability.

Write down your initial thoughts when you think of vulnerability. Can you identify the voice behind the thoughts? Who is it that is judging you? A parent? A partner? A teacher? Someone else who holds meaning for you?

____

____

____

____

____

____

____

Advantages of Vulnerability:

Vulnerability is the wellspring of creativity, love, authenticity, and joy. For centuries, art and literature have depicted this state not as a collapse, but as a revelation: the moment a guard drops to reveal who we truly are. This exposure is daunting, which is precisely why we mistake it for weakness when it is, in fact, the bedrock of courage.

When we allow ourselves to be vulnerable, we cease contorting to please others. We invite empathy, for in lowering our own barriers, we make it simpler to comprehend and share genuine sentiment, giving others permission to do the same. This exchange fosters a deeper compassion, a readiness to pardon, and a capacity for true embrace.

Fundamentally, vulnerability is emotional integrity. It allows us to move through our feelings rather than wall them off, which is the cornerstone of mental and emotional well-being. It is a declaration of bravery: in accepting and admitting what we are experiencing, we grow resilient and bold. In relationships, vulnerability acts as the ultimate litmus test and bonding agent. It helps us identify those who will embrace our true selves. By leading through example, our own openness gives others the safety to be open in return, forging connections of immense strength.

Vulnerability is an inescapable aspect of a life fully lived. The choice is not whether we will encounter it, but how we will meet it. We can fight it, or we can welcome it as the force that deepens every meaningful experience. Consider the courage required to say "I love you" first, to try something profoundly new, or to share a private struggle. Our instinct may be to shun these risks, but perseverance within them unlocks a profound reward: a life lived not as a performance, but with authentic, unguarded truth.

As valuable as vulnerability is, it can leave us emotionally tender. Knowing how to protect your energy is therefore essential, ensuring you can continue to show up fully without being depleted.

Life often pulls us in countless directions. Between career, education, family, and countless other responsibilities, moments for oneself can feel scarce. This is especially true for those in helping professions—the social worker, the stay-at-home parent, the nurse, and the teacher—who may devote so much of themselves to others that by day's end, they feel utterly drained.

There are days when it seems everyone you know is facing a crisis, and you are their sole confidant. While the desire to help is a profound part of our nature, the compulsion to be perpetually present for everyone is unsustainable. We are conditioned to alleviate the suffering of those we care about, yet in our devotion to their needs, we often neglect our own physical and emotional requirements, which are just as vital.

To the outside world, your energy may seem limitless, but beneath a cheerful exterior often lies deep fatigue. The truth is, you cannot be everyone's constant support. To attempt this is a sure path to burnout, leaving you unable to help anyone, including yourself. The alternative is to consciously cultivate practices that preserve your inner reserves.

Establish Strong Boundaries: This vital act of self-care is often difficult. Those accustomed to your constant availability, family or friends, may initially react with irritation. This reaction is natural; hold your ground. In time, they will adjust. Your presence can remain steadfast, yet your message must be clear: you are there for them, but you cannot shoulder their emotional, physical, or temporal responsibilities for them. They must learn to carry their own weight.

Make Time for Yourself: You are not obligated to be perpetually on call. Consider deliberately disconnecting—switching your phone off for a period and learning to enjoy solitude. Distinguish this healthy solitude from isolation or withdrawal. If loneliness surfaces, that is a signal to seek connection, perhaps from a mental health professional or trusted loved ones, not a reason to abandon your necessary boundaries.

Acknowledge Your Feelings: Those in caregiving roles become masters of compartmentalization, expertly setting their own feelings aside to hold space for others. The danger lies in becoming so proficient at turning your emotions off that you forget to switch them back on. Unfelt feelings do not vanish; they migrate into the body, often manifesting as persistent soreness or tension. The body keeps a perfect record of every emotion you shove away. Common areas for storing this stress and unresolved trauma are the hips and pelvis, where prior injuries and emotional history can lodge themselves physically.

Listen to Your Body's Signals: To reduce negative exposure, become attuned to these physical messages. If you feel discomfort in a conversation steeped in gossip, judgment, or complaint, you are not required to manufacture an excuse. You may simply excuse yourself and leave. Of course, this is not always possible or appropriate, especially with a loved one. In those cases, the opportunity shifts to mindful engagement: you can be vulnerably honest about the impact of the negativity, validate their feelings without adopting them, and permit yourself small breaks from the draining discussion.

This is a practice. Some days, immersing yourself in the positive will feel challenging. In those moments, the essential reminder is this: while you cannot control the world or others' responses, your power resides in how you choose to react. This is the core of protecting your energy—curating your inner world amidst the chaos of the outer one.

Exercise: Practice, practice, practice doing regular body scans. Start by closing your eyes to scan your body, starting from the crown of your head, moving slowly through your body to the tips of your toes. Write down below what you felt and where.

What emotions are you feeling?

What do you feel?

What do you see?

Discuss the feeling.

Reflect on the shift. There is often a palpable lightness that follows the honest expression of long-held feelings. This is the mechanism of release at work: the more you courageously address these emotions, the less control they hold over you.

Integrating this awareness into daily life requires simple, tangible practices. One method is to create a ritual of shared check-ins. For instance, a couple might place a dry-erase board by their entryway, pausing upon returning home to briefly scan and note their emotional and physical state. Such a practice fosters mutual mindfulness, transforming raw sensitivity into a structured form of supportive empathy. It does not diminish one's sensitivity; rather, it channels that perceptive ability toward deeper self-understanding and a clearer, more compassionate view of the other's inner world.

Ultimately, sensitivity is not a weakness to be managed but a profound form of attunement to be mastered. Your capacity to tune into the nuanced feelings of others grants you a rare insight. This is not a comic book superpower but a deeply human strength: an ability to perceive what is often unspoken and to respond with genuine kindness and understanding. In a world that often prizes detachment, this quality is not a liability but a formidable asset for forging authentic connections.

Notes for Chapter 9

Key Takeaways

- **Being sensitive isn't something bad.**
- **Hypersensitivity has its advantages as well.**
- **Being sensitive is all about being able to feel someone's happiness and distress as your own, and how you can turn that into something positive through compassion and care.**
- **Being an empath is being able to perceive the emotions and moods in the ambiance and people.**
- **The stigma attached to vulnerability equating to bearing weakness is false. Vulnerability is a strength.**
- **Vulnerability allows you to remain true to yourself, keeping you from becoming someone that you're not just to fit in or gain approval from others.**
- **While all this is a good thing, you have to be careful to make sure no one takes advantage of you being a natural caregiver.**

Chapter 10: Perspective

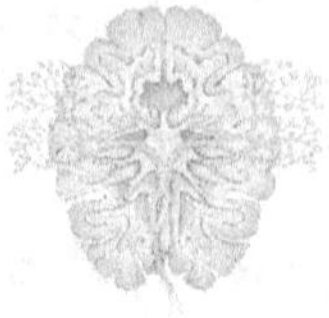

"Not everything that can be counted counts, and not everything that counts can be counted."

-Albert Einstein

This single observation reframes a fundamental question: What truly counts? The answers are as varied as human experience, yet they consistently point inward, toward character and impact. One perspective emphasizes personal values, suggesting we define ourselves not by status, income, or appearance, but by our generosity, kindness, and compassion.

Another measures a life by its external ripple, arguing that our significance is determined by the difference we make in the lives of others. A third focuses on the resilience of the spirit, where what counts is not a final success or a fatal failure, but the enduring courage to continue. Each of these views challenges the superficial metrics often mistaken for substance.

What Matters Most: Living A Meaningful Life

Life holds profound beauty and deep trepidation. While we aspire to serenity, it is often in the crucible of adversity that we confront and sometimes answer our most significant questions. Yet we should not reserve this inquiry for times of pain; to ask these questions in moments of peace is to build resilience for the inevitable storms. A modern tendency is to dodge discomfort and delay this vital introspection, seeing it as inconvenient. This avoidance, however, only weakens our capacity to navigate future suffering, which remains an inescapable part of the human journey. The challenge is to harness these difficult times, a task made harder in an age that often prioritizes immediate pleasure and carefully curated public perfection.

Many philosophies and worldviews are built around the aim of alleviating human suffering. Yet a recurring insight across traditions is that a degree of struggle is integral to a purposeful and felt life. Pain can carve the channels through which we later experience profound joy and appreciation.

Consider existentialism, which places the responsibility for creating meaning squarely on the individual. This philosophy does not deny suffering but proposes that by confronting our absolute freedom and making conscious choices within it, we can forge a personal purpose. This self-authored meaning, in turn, becomes a bulwark against the anxieties of an uncertain world and overwhelming emotions like fear.

This abstract idea becomes clear through example.

- **Believing in individual choice and the freedom to make decisions that shape one′s life.**
- **Holding the belief that you can choose your own meaning of life rather than adhering to predetermined or societal expectations.**
- **Knowing that our actions demonstrate our choices and always concern matters within our power to choose, we should be deliberate about things that are within our control and are attainable through our actions.**
- **Experiencing existential despair or anguish when confronted with the overwhelming task of defining one′s own existence and purpose.**

What Can You Do to Prepare Yourself for Suffering?

The first step in navigating life's inevitable surprises is not to predict every pitfall, but to cultivate a mindful awareness that happiness is not a permanent state to be taken for granted, but a fleeting gift to be recognized.

From this awareness follows a crucial task: we must discover something worth enduring for. A personally resonant meaning or a clear objective enables us to withstand pain that would otherwise be meaningless and crushing. It is often in hindsight that we discern value in our trials, not because the suffering itself was good, but because our passage through it forged resilience, clarified our priorities, or revealed the true nature of those around us. The temporary hurt can, at times, yield a long-term strengthening of character or understanding.

This process hinges on our most fundamental power: the choice of response. Even in the darkest circumstances, we are not required to adopt foolish optimism. The "good" we might discover could be as simple and profound as the clear-eyed recognition of who stands with us in authentic concern, and who remains only a fair-weather companion.

Why Can't We Just Concentrate on Being Happy?

"Happiness is a choice, not a result. Nothing will make you happy until you choose to be happy."

-Ralph Marston

This popular sentiment contains a partial truth, yet focusing on happiness as a primary goal is often counterproductive. Lasting happiness tends to emerge as a byproduct of engagement in worthwhile tasks and relationships, not as the direct result of a decision or the pursuit of a continuous sensation.

The relationship between choice and happiness is complex. While we cannot simply decide to feel joy, we can make choices that cultivate the conditions where happiness is more likely to take root. Research suggests our baseline is influenced by a mix of genetics, circumstances, and critically, our intentional activities and outlook. This is where our agency lies: in the daily choices that shape our experience. We can train our neural pathways through practice, by consciously cultivating gratitude, by seeking perspective, and by engaging in acts of kindness. These are not instant fixes, but deliberate orientations that, over time, build a mind more inclined to recognize and resonate with happiness.

When my client, Mr. R., came to me for therapy, he was going through a rough patch in his life. The fifty-six-year-old architect came to me eighteen months after losing his wife to cancer, his career to industry downturn, and his home to foreclosure. Those were quite painful situations for anyone to handle.

"I used to be someone. I was a partner in a respected firm. I had a beautiful marriage. We had a home we'd spent twenty years making perfect. I knew exactly who I was. And in the span of two years, every single piece of that is gone."

He described waking up in a rented room in his brother's house. During that testing time, he was unable to find a single reason to get out of bed. "People say things like 'this too shall pass' or 'everything happens for a reason.' They're trying to help. But it's insulting. Nothing about this has meaning. It's just loss stacked on loss. I'm fifty-six years old, and I cannot imagine starting over from zero. I cannot for the life of me figure out why I should even bother starting over."

That was one of the most devastating forms of existential crisis I had come across in quite a while. After losing the structures that gave his life shape, he was left staring into a void with no direction. We talked about stories of people who had lost everything at some point in life and then built themselves from scratch.

Mr. R. was not impressed initially.

"What did you do this morning?" I asked.

He looked confused by the question. "I got up. Made coffee. Went for a walk because I didn't have anywhere else to be."

"Why did you get up?"

Long silence. "I don't know. Habit, I guess."

"And the coffee?"

"I like coffee."

"And the walk?"

"The air was good. The light was good. I saw a heron by the pond that I'd never seen there before."

We sat with that for a moment. "You got up because you could. You made coffee because it gave you pleasure. You walked because the morning was beautiful, and you noticed a heron. Those are not grand existential purposes. But they're small, tangible reasons to continue. We find meaning, again and again, in the smallest available opportunity."

The work that followed was not about finding a sweeping narrative that redeemed his losses. It was about practicing, daily, the act of finding one small thing worth doing. Some days it was as simple as "the morning light through the window." Some days it was "my brother made his terrible scrambled eggs, and we laughed about them." Some days it was "I sketched something just to see if I still could."

"I'm not going to tell you I've found grand purpose," he said six months into our work. "I haven't. My wife is still gone. My career is still over. I'm still rebuilding from rubble. But I'm not staring at the ceiling anymore, waiting to not exist. I'm here. And most days, that's enough."

In A Hedonistic World, How Do We Find Meaning?

As discussed, the significance of a person's existence is profoundly individual. While religion can provide a shared framework, meaning in the modern world is often forged in three primary arenas: meaningful work, deep connections with loved ones, and the lessons carved by suffering through difficult times.

Life has a way of delivering abrupt, shocking awakenings: a global crisis, the loss of a loved one, a shattered relationship, a natural disaster, or a vanished career. In the unstable aftermath of such events, a terrible clarity often emerges, illuminating what actually matters. We vow in those raw moments never to forget the insight, never to return to our old, unconscious ways. Yet the central challenge is precisely that: staying awake.

However profound the imprint, time has a quiet, erosive power. The urgent clarity fades. The familiar delusions, where our mental projections masquerade as reality, slowly seep back in, diluted but persistent. So, within a fast-paced society brimming with distraction and false progress, how do we hold onto what truly counts? How do we resist the seductive, familiar jumble of our own repetitive thoughts and feelings, which so often lead us back into needless suffering?

Maintaining the clarity of what truly matters requires deliberate, ongoing practices that counter the world's noise and our own forgetful nature. These are not tasks to be completed, but orientations to be cultivated.

First, capture clarity when it strikes. The moment a piercing insight arrives, record it in a dedicated journal. Return to these entries regularly; let your own past wisdom remind you of truths the present may obscure.

Translate insight into action. If a revelation shows that certain pursuits are empty, have the courage to adjust your lifestyle accordingly. Let your behavior reflect your understanding.

Curate your influences. Regularly immerse yourself in media, audio, writing, and film: that reinforces a broader, more inspired perspective. Create a personal anthology of works that resonate with your deepest values, returning to them as a touchstone.

Define your purpose. Draft a personal manifesto or mission statement. Place this concise expression of your core principles where you will encounter it daily, allowing it to act as a silent, persistent guide.

Embrace the power of commitment. Consider making a solemn, personal vow. This ancient practice cuts through ambivalence, creating a solid internal promise to yourself about who you wish to be and what you intend to honor.

Cultivate silence and solitude. Regularly create space for quiet reflection. In the absence of external stimulus, you can hear your own inner voice and discern if your daily path aligns with your stated direction.

Contemplate impermanence. Ask yourself how your priorities would shift if your time were sharply limited. The awareness of life's fragility has a singular power to strip away trivial concerns, burning through the absurdity of our petty compulsions to reveal the substance beneath.

Practice mindful awareness. Meditation is not merely a tool for stress reduction; it is the foundational practice for remembering what matters. It trains the mind to observe thoughts without being swept away by them, creating the mental space to choose your response from a place of clarity, not reaction.

Forge an authentic community. Intentionally spend time with people who see you, who share your values, and who inspire you to live a purposeful life. Their presence is a living reminder and a source of strength.

It is dangerously easy to become reabsorbed by the routine. Staying awake, making choices from conscious awareness rather than conditioned habit, demands tenacity, strategy, and a committed practice of remembering.

What are you giving high importance to? What counts to you right now?

What do you want to count to you?

It is essential to bring this reflective awareness into our social interactions. As social creatures, our communication and connections directly shape our sense of belonging, security, and self-concept.

Navigating this requires a balance of conviction and humility. Just when our own perspective feels settled, an encounter with another's radically different viewpoint can remind us that our understanding is always partial. This is not a cause for frustration, but an opportunity. The disciplined practice of listening, truly listening, to opinions that seem foreign or challenging, prevents our worldview from hardening into dogma. By leaving room for the diverse, even unsettling perspectives of others, we allow our own journey to be challenged, expanded, and enriched in unexpected ways.

Respecting Others' Opinions and Perspectives

A common impulse, especially in polarized environments, is to treat a difference of perspective as a conflict to be won. The goal shifts from understanding to dominance, often accompanied by hostility intended to humiliate the other side. This approach is not only corrosive to discourse but is ultimately ineffective for anyone seeking genuine growth.

When faced with disagreement, aggression or passive-aggression are choices, not necessities. The more productive path is to engage in dialogue. Recognizing that life is complex and rarely yields to a single interpretation allows you to approach another's viewpoint not as a threat, but as a potential source of insight. The person you disagree with has lived a different life, which naturally shapes a different understanding of the world.

The objective, therefore, is not to assert your opinion while dismissing theirs, but to first seek comprehension. Ask clarifying questions. Listen intently. Then, paraphrase their point of view back to them, not as a performative tactic, but to ensure you have truly understood. This act demonstrates respect and intellectual generosity; it does not signify agreement or defeat.

True growth occurs not by reinforcing your existing positions, but by unearthing new considerations and challenging your own assumptions. While some may argue in bad faith, most people disagree from a place of genuine, if different, conviction. By resisting the urge to respond strongly to every differing perspective, you preserve the emotional and mental space necessary to discern which engagements are worth your energy and which are best met with quiet disengagement.

The Do's and Don'ts

There are many constructive methods to make disagreement work for you, and conflicts are a terrific chance for disagreement, approached constructively, and can become a powerful catalyst for growth rather than a source of conflict. The key is to shift the objective from winning to understanding.

Effective engagement begins with a foundation of respect. Communicate your viewpoint calmly, focusing on facts over volatile emotions. Remember, you are disagreeing with a specific idea, not launching a personal attack on the individual. To build rapport, first acknowledge any neutral ground or shared goals; this establishes camaraderie before navigating the points of difference.

Language is crucial. Frame your perspective with "I" statements ("I see it this way...") to avoid sounding accusatory. Your primary task is to listen actively, ensuring you comprehend the other person's main arguments, not just their opening salvo. This requires suspending your internal rebuttal while they speak.

Maintain an open mind with the genuine belief that you might learn something. Research unfamiliar points they raise. If the discussion becomes aggressive or unproductive, be prepared to disengage civilly; aggression only breeds more aggression and closes all doors to insight.

The pitfalls to avoid are as important as the practices to adopt. Never make the disagreement personal by demeaning the other person. Reject the assumption that you are automatically correct; the truth often lies between perspectives. Avoid a closed-minded stance that seeks only to confirm pre-existing beliefs. While you should not fear sincere disagreement, it is more valuable than false harmony, you must also discern when a conversation has ceased to be a dialogue and is no longer a worthy investment of your energy. Ultimately, progress hinges on your willingness to broaden your thinking to incorporate previously unconsidered viewpoints, even if you ultimately integrate them selectively, collaboration and personal growth. Seek points of agreement to establish some areas of agreement, and then learn more about the points of contention with the other party. Just because you disagree with something doesn't mean you have to respond with hate and hostility.

Exercise: Do some personal soul searching: How do you disagree with others? Do you play nice? Do you feel offended or upset? How do you usually feel after a disagreement?

____

____

____

____

____

What would you like to change about your communication to disagree differently, and how would that affect your relationships? How would it make you feel at the end of a disagreement?

Nonviolent Communication (NVC)

Nonviolent Communication (NVC) is a sophisticated framework for communication, rooted in the principles of nonviolence and humanistic psychology. Developed by clinical psychologist Marshall Rosenberg in the mid-20th century, its core objective is to increase empathy and compassion, thereby improving the quality of connection rather than simply ending disagreements.

The approach is founded on a powerful premise: when people feel truly heard, it becomes easier to arrive at solutions that fulfill everyone's basic needs. This eliminates the necessity for force or manipulation. NVC provides a structured method to achieve this, based on four components: observing without judging, clearly expressing feelings and needs, and making empathetic, actionable requests.

Our communication is expressed through far more than words; it is carried in tone, expression, and posture. NVC encourages bringing conscious, positive intention to these signals. This means adopting an open, non-threatening posture, softening one's vocal tone, and choosing words that connect rather than alienate. As a listener, the practice involves reflective listening, paraphrasing what you've heard to confirm understanding, and the disciplined patience to not interrupt.

At its heart, NVC addresses a universal human longing: to be heard, seen, and understood. We can meet this need in others through empathetic listening, validation, and loving speech. Inevitably, emotions will sometimes run high. In such moments, a critical NVC practice is to honestly communicate the need for a pause to state that the conversation is important, but that you require a brief break to regain composure and return with a clear, rational mind. This temporary withdrawal is not avoidance, but a responsible strategy to protect the quality of the dialogue.

Suppose you need to communicate a hurt feeling. The framing is critical. Contrast the statement "I feel unheard when I speak and don't get a response," with "You aren't listening to me." The first is an expression of personal experience; the second is an accusation that virtually guarantees a defensive reply, sparking a conflict that ensures your underlying need for connection will go unmet. This is the discipline of NVC: to own our emotions and articulate our needs without implicitly blaming the other.

Consider a common domestic tension. If a loved one says, "You never help me. I do everything. You don't even care," the listener feels attacked and will likely retaliate with a defensive list of their own contributions. The communication has failed.

Now, imagine the same need expressed differently: "I'm feeling overwhelmed and would really love some help in the kitchen right now." This statement, free of accusation and focused on a present, actionable request, invites cooperation rather than conflict. The conscious effort to frame needs around "I" and avoid the accusatory "you" can fundamentally alter the emotional climate of an interaction.

Nonviolent Communication has proven its value beyond theory; it is applied in clinical psychotherapy and taught in workshops worldwide as a practical method for resolving conflict, improving relationships, and fostering harmony in both personal and professional spheres.

NOTE: Now is a good time to go online, purchase an NVC training course, and begin practicing the art of NVC.

Notes for Chapter 10

Key Takeaways

- **What really counts is living a meaningful life.**
- **You can always choose to be happy.**
- **Respecting others' perspectives is a must for self-growth.**
- **Hearing others' opinions is important in order to learn something new.**
- **Tolerance of others' perspectives doesn't mean you are losing an argument or agreeing with them.**
- **One needs to maintain honest disagreement instead of fake peace.**
- **Embrace empathy and warmth for everyone around.**
- **Avoid getting into unnecessary conflicts.**
- **Nonviolent communication training to learn and practice the art of productive communication, such as listening and validating using gentle words.**

Chapter 11: What Kind of Romantic Relationship Do You Want?

NOTE: There are too many types of romantic relationships to cover in one chapter, so we will cover just the basics. If you aren't interested in a relationship or what you are seeking or experiencing isn't here, feel free to skip this chapter.

Romantic relationships are not a monolithic experience. A diverse spectrum of partnerships exists, each appealing to different individuals or to the same individual at different phases of life. Our receptiveness to various relationship structures is heavily influenced by our current circumstances, maturity, and core personal needs.

Therefore, a crucial step is to move beyond assumed defaults. This involves recognizing the varied forms relationships can take, understanding the inherent benefits and challenges of each, and engaging in honest introspection about your own authentic wants and requirements. From this clarified self-awareness, you can then seek a compatible partner who desires a similar connection or initiate a vital conversation with an existing partner to ensure you share a mutual vision for the partnership.

Independent Relationship

In an independent relationship, both partners maintain significant autonomy. They often spend considerable time apart, pursuing personal interests and activities separate from their partner. This structure thrives on a foundation of high confidence and trust, where time spent separately or on different hobbies is not viewed with skepticism, but as natural expressions of individual identity.

The greatest strength of this dynamic is the mutual empowerment it fosters. Two self-sufficient individuals understand intuitively that to preserve their own freedom, they must genuinely grant it to their partner. This creates a climate of respect and non-possessiveness.

The primary challenge lies in the perception of emotional distance. If one partner is perpetually engaged in their own world without demonstrating interest in the other's life, feelings of neglect or irrelevance can surface. This risk is amplified when one partner is inherently more autonomous, and the other leans toward a more connective, interdependent style. Clear, ongoing communication about emotional needs is therefore critical to ensure neither person feels forgotten.

Ultimately, a thriving independent relationship is not about the absence of connection, but about a conscious balance. It requires finding the equilibrium where autonomy is preserved without sacrificing empathy, mutual involvement, and thoughtful compromise, the hallmarks of a healthy *interdependence*.

Ms. B., a thirty-nine-year-old software engineer, came to therapy at the insistence of her partner of four years. She only agreed to seek help when her partner threatened to leave unless they "figured this out."

Initially, she looked confused when she told me that her partner says that she doesn't love him.

"I do love him. I just don't understand why loving someone means I have to see them every single day, text constantly, or spend all my free time together. I have my own life. I have friends, hobbies, and work I care about. He takes that as evidence that I don't care about the relationship. I take his need for constant contact as controlling. We're stuck."

It is a common issue that many couples face in their relationship. As we explored their dynamic, two perfectly valid but incompatible relationship styles emerged. Ms. B. was wired for what we'd call an independent relationship. She needed significant autonomy, valued time alone, and experienced excessive togetherness as suffocating rather than loving. Her partner, raised in a close-knit family where connection meant constant presence, experienced time apart as abandonment and distance as rejection.

"Neither of you is wrong," I told her.

"That's what makes it so frustrating. I'm not being distant because I don't care. That's just how I function best. And I know that his being clingy is his way of showing love. But we can't both get what we need. Someone has to compromise, and whoever does is going to be miserable."

This is the particular pain of style mismatch. It is not a failure of love, but a fundamental incompatibility in how love is expressed and experienced.

We did something that made Ms. B. uncomfortable: we examined what she actually wanted in a partnership, independent of this particular relationship. "If you could design your ideal relationship without considering his needs," I asked, "what would it look like?"

She thought for a long time. "I'd want a partner who has their own full life. Who doesn't need me to be their primary source of entertainment or emotional regulation? Someone I see a few times a week intentionally, where the time together is genuinely chosen and valued, not obligatory. Where we can go days without contact and trust that we're still solid. Where independence isn't interpreted as distance but as respect for each other's wholeness."

"And when you describe that to your partner?"

"He says it sounds lonely. He says it sounds like we're roommates who occasionally date, not partners building a life together."

We brought her partner in for a joint session. His ideal was different but equally valid: daily connection, integrated lives, shared routines, being each other's primary person. That relationship structure felt like home to him.

"Can either of you be happy in the other's ideal relationship?" I asked them both directly.

The silence was long and heavy.

"No," her partner said finally. "I can try. I have been trying. But I'm lonely all the time in this relationship, and that's not sustainable. I don't want to be the person who needs less than I need, but I also can't keep pretending I'm okay with this much distance."

"I can't be the person who needs less space than I need," Ms. B. said quietly. "I've tried. I feel like I'm suffocating. And then I resent him for something that isn't his fault."

They ended the relationship three weeks later. They loved each other enough to acknowledge that their fundamental relational needs were incompatible. It was one of the most mature, painful endings I've witnessed.

"We're both fine. We're just not fine together. I need to find someone whose independence needs match mine. He needs to find someone whose connection needs match his. Love isn't enough if the structure doesn't work."

Sometimes, the best decision you can make is to walk away from a relationship that cannot meet your fundamental needs, even when love is present.

Yet while some relationships struggle because partners require too much independence from one another, others face the opposite problem, where the need for connection becomes so overwhelming that personal boundaries and autonomy begin to disappear. In clinical terms, we call it a co-dependent relationship.

Co-dependent Relationship

A co-dependent relationship represents a dysfunctional extreme, not a simple counterpart to healthy independence. In this dynamic, partners are enmeshed, relying on each other for an excessive degree of emotional validation and identity. A co-dependent individual may feel incapable of functioning or making decisions without their partner, and they typically prioritize the relationship's harmony and their partner's needs above their own to an unhealthy degree.

While this can create an intense sense of closeness and a propensity for compromise, the cost is the erosion of the self. Individuals in co-dependent partnerships risk completely losing sight of their own desires, needs, and individuality, deriving their worth almost exclusively from the role of caretaker or approved partner.

The hallmarks of this dynamic include poor boundaries, a fear of abandonment that fuels possessiveness or jealousy, and a reluctance to spend time apart. Therefore, the prescribed remedy is not to "balance" the co-dependency, but to actively dismantle it. This requires deliberately creating space for self-reflection and independent activity, not as a relational tactic, but as a necessary act of reclaiming one's own identity. Professional therapy is often crucial to untangle the underlying patterns of low self-worth and fear that drive the enmeshment.

It is critical to distinguish co-dependency from healthy interdependence. A successful, close relationship is built on two whole individuals choosing to connect, not on two halves needing to merge to feel complete. The goal is not to manage co-dependence, but to grow out of it into a state of secure, autonomous connection.

Open Relationship

An open relationship, falling under the broader category of consensual non-monogamy, is one in which partners agree that each may engage in sexual or romantic connections with other people. These arrangements are highly varied and defined by the specific agreements between the partners involved.

Some couples maintain a clear primary partnership, permitting outside sexual encounters but not deep romantic entanglements. Others may allow for multiple romantic and sexual connections, sometimes without a hierarchical "primary" label. Some monogamous couples may also experiment with temporary openness due to circumstance.

Successful open relationships are built on an exceptional foundation of trust, self-awareness, and meticulous, ongoing communication. For those suited to it, this structure can provide a great deal of fulfillment, exploring connections and sexuality without the constraints of monogamy.

However, this model is not without significant challenges. It demands a high degree of emotional security to manage jealousy. It can complicate the deepening of singular, intimate bonds that many seek in romance. Crucially, it is not an "extreme" form of independence, nor a solution for a failing monogamous relationship. It is a distinct relational choice that requires absolute honesty, first with oneself about one's own needs and capacities, and then with one's partner. Agreeing to non-monogamy out of fear or appeasement, rather than genuine alignment, is a recipe for profound hurt and the relationship's collapse.

Long-Distance Relationship

A long-distance relationship is defined by partners living in separate geographical locations. Its success depends less on the exact miles between them and more on the strength of their connection and the clarity of their mutual goal.

This structure often works best for two self-sufficient individuals deeply committed to a shared future. It is frequently a practical choice for couples separated by education, career, military service, or family obligations. The distance can provide a unique space for personal growth and focus on individual goals, all while maintaining an emotional bond.

The foundation of a successful long-distance relationship is deliberate, consistent communication and the creation of shared rituals, whether daily calls or scheduled virtual dates. However, significant challenges are inherent. The physical absence can strain local social lives and create a sense of living in two places at once. Jealousy or anxiety can arise from the fear of a partner building a fulfilling daily life that feels exclusive. Crucially, both partners must be explicitly aligned on the relationship's boundaries and its ultimate trajectory. A defined plan or end date for closing the distance is often essential for sustaining hope and commitment. While some long-distance couples may mutually agree to open the relationship, this is a complex decision that must be reached through explicit, honest dialogue; it is never an assumption or a default response to loneliness. Without profound trust, clear communication, and a shared vision, the distance can become a chasm.

A Just-For-Now Relationship

A 'just for now' relationship is a mutual understanding for a short-term, low-commitment romantic engagement. It often includes physical intimacy and romantic affection, but both parties consciously do not frame it within a long-term future.

These relationships can offer enjoyment and companionship without the deeper investment and complexity of a committed partnership. They may suit individuals who desire romantic connection but lack the time, energy, or current life alignment for a long-term commitment. Clear, upfront communication about this transient nature is paramount to prevent mismatched expectations and emotional injury.

The inherent challenge of this dynamic is its potential instability. The very lack of a profound emotional foundation can cause it to dissipate quickly. Conversely, sustained physical intimacy and time spent together can naturally foster deeper feelings, complicating the original agreement. If one partner develops significantly more affection than the other, the arrangement becomes fraught. Therefore, regular, honest check-ins about each person's satisfaction and ongoing expectations are essential. While a 'just for now' relationship can, on rare occasion, evolve into something more serious as a genuine connection deepens, this should never be the unspoken hope or strategy at its outset. Entering such a dynamic requires absolute clarity and honesty with oneself and the other person about its defined, limited scope.

Physical Relationship

A purely sexual or physical relationship focuses exclusively on physical intimacy, deliberately excluding romantic emotional attachment. These arrangements are based on a mutual understanding that the connection exists to fulfill physical needs without the expectation of emotional bonding or long-term commitment.

Such relationships can suit individuals who are clear about their desire for physical connection without emotional entanglement, or those in *consensually* open relationships where such external encounters are agreed upon. Crucially, they are not a tool for infidelity; honesty and consent with all involved parties are non-negotiable.

The central challenge is the innate human tendency for physical intimacy to spark emotional attachment. Therefore, explicit, ongoing communication about boundaries and the nature of the connection is critical to prevent painful mismatches in expectation. This dynamic is not viable for everyone, as many people find physical and emotional intimacy inextricably linked. Before engaging in such an arrangement, rigorous self-honesty is required. You must assess whether you can genuinely compartmentalize in this way. When entered with clear-eyed mutual consent and self-awareness, a physical relationship can be satisfying. However, if maintaining the boundary requires suppressing or denying developing emotions, the personal cost ultimately outweighs the fleeting benefit.

The story of Ms. J., a thirty-six-year-old physician who sought relationship consultancy, illustrates this dynamic more clearly. She was on the verge of accepting her boyfriend's marriage proposal, yet found herself unsettled by an unexpected emotional response.

"He's perfect on paper," she told me. "Successful, kind, stable, reliable. My family loves him. He'd be an excellent father. We never fight. We agree on all the important things. I should be thrilled. Instead, I'm just... numb."

As we began working together, I introduced Sternberg's framework: passion, intimacy, and commitment—not as a diagnostic label, but as a way to explore what might be present, what might be blocked, and what might still be possible to build.

"Let's take this slowly," I said. "What does closeness look like between the two of you?"

She hesitated. "We talk. We function well. But I don't share my deeper fears or uncertainties. He's very logical, very straightforward. I've always felt... it would be too much for him. So I keep those parts to myself."

Rather than concluding that intimacy was absent, we explored what might be inhibiting it. Over the following weeks, our work focused on helping her experiment with vulnerability—gradually expressing more of her internal world, noticing his responses, and challenging her assumptions about how he might receive her.

At the same time, we examined their communication patterns. Much of their interaction, she realized, was efficient but emotionally neutral. There was little space for curiosity, playfulness, or emotional risk. Together, we worked on expanding those moments—encouraging her to move beyond functional conversations into more personal, emotionally engaged exchanges.

When we turned to passion, she initially described it as entirely absent. But rather than treating attraction as something fixed, we explored the conditions under which desire can emerge. We looked at routine, predictability, and the absence of novelty in their relationship. She acknowledged that their dynamic had become structured and practical early on, leaving little room for spontaneity or emotional tension.

We also considered her own internal landscape—her beliefs about relationships, her timeline for marriage and children, and the quiet pressure she felt to "choose well" rather than "feel deeply." These factors, too, can dampen emotional and physical engagement.

Importantly, this phase of the work was not about deciding whether the relationship was viable, but about actively testing whether greater intimacy and connection could be cultivated. She made deliberate efforts: initiating more emotionally open conversations, suggesting new shared experiences, and allowing herself to be seen in ways she had previously avoided.

Over time, however, a clearer picture began to emerge—not from assumption, but from experience. Despite increased vulnerability, improved communication, and conscious efforts to shift the relational dynamic, she found that her emotional and physical responses remained largely unchanged.

"I understand him better now," she said at one point. "And I think he understands me more than I gave him credit for. But something still doesn't move in me. It feels... steady, but not alive."

Only after this process did we revisit Sternberg's model—not as a prescription, but as a reflection. What she described was a relationship grounded strongly in commitment, with some growing capacity for intimacy, but a persistent absence of passion.

"You're not reacting to a lack of effort," I told her. "You're responding to what remained after the effort."

This distinction mattered. The decision she faced was no longer about whether she had "tried hard enough," but about whether the relationship, as it genuinely existed, was enough for her.

"No," she said quietly. "It isn't. And I hate that it isn't."

Ending the relationship was not an impulsive rejection of something imperfect, but the result of sustained engagement, exploration, and emotional work. Nothing was fundamentally wrong, yet something essential was missing.

A relationship requires shared effort; both partners must be willing to invest time and emotional energy into its growth.

In many cases, what feels like a lack of "spark" can be traced to modifiable factors: communication patterns, emotional safety, unexamined expectations, or the weight of routine.

In therapy, we often focus on identifying and addressing these barriers. We try our best to help partners communicate more openly, rebuild emotional intimacy, introduce novelty, and understand the individual histories that shape how they relate to one another.

In some cases, these shifts can meaningfully transform the relationship, allowing both intimacy and passion to emerge or re-emerge. In others, as in Ms. J.'s experience, the process brings clarity rather than change. When genuine effort does not alter the underlying emotional reality, the absence of connection may not be a problem to solve, but a truth to acknowledge.

While no theory can perfectly capture the fluid complexity of human connection, Sternberg's model provides a valuable vocabulary for reflection. It allows us to assess what elements are strongly present, which may be underdeveloped, and where we might wish to focus our nurturing energy. To apply this, consider your current or a past relationship. Reflect on the balance of passion, intimacy, and commitment that defined it. This act of categorization is not about assigning a fixed label, but about illuminating the structure of your connection to better understand its strengths and potential gaps.

Relationship Role Assessment Worksheet focused on Dynamic Alignment

Who are you in your relationship? (If this doesn't pertain to where you are in life right now, it's okay! You can come back to it when it does.)

____

____

____

____

____

____

____

Analyze your relationship and yourself as the one half of the couple you make. Sit down with your partner and discuss the dynamics of your relationship before answering the following questions. (If you are not in a relationship, it would be fun to fill this out in accordance to whom you want to be and be with)

How would you describe who you are in your relationship? (Identify: Expectations, Meanings, and Dynamics; it may affect how you perform in your role)

____

____

____

How would you describe your role in your relationship? (Role linked to your position in the relationship: Partner, Friend, Parent, Teacher, Housekeeper, Chef, etc.)

How would your partner describe who you are and your role in your relationship?

How has this person changed from what he/she was at the beginning of your relationship?

Who do you want to be? What role do you want to have?

Who do you want your partner to be? What role do you want him/her/they/them to have?

Are you happy with who you are in your relationship?

Are you happy with who your partner is in your relationship?

Write down some points or a potential conversation you want to have with your partner.

Did communication help you find better ground? How do you feel after your discussion?

Being in a new relationship can be hard to manage. Setting ground rules for it may help you both realize your boundaries and follow them, thus improving both your lives and the relationship. While every relationship is unique, successful partnerships across all stages tend to be anchored by common, conscious practices. These are not rigid rules, but guiding principles that foster security and growth.

In new relationships, the focus should be on discovery and pacing. This involves granting each other space to maintain individuality, integrating respectfully into each other's social worlds, and asking foundational questions about values and life goals with kindness and curiosity—not as an interrogation, but as a mutual exploration. It requires balancing the thrill of a new connection with the wisdom of observing a partner's character over time.

As a relationship deepens into consistency, the practices evolve. They center on reliable emotional presence, honoring shared plans, engaging with each other's separate worlds (friends, family, work), and actively learning each other's specific languages of love and appreciation. The bond is maintained through the daily choice to share experiences, both significant and mundane.

The step into cohabitation introduces a practical dimension that must be harmonized with the emotional one. Success hinges on explicit, preemptive agreements about finances and domestic responsibilities to prevent resentment. It demands a mutual clarity of purpose for sharing a home and a commitment to navigate the inevitable friction that arises when the "honeymoon" ambiance fades, seeing these moments as growing pains to be sorted out together with respect for both shared space and individual need.

Marriage, as the most formalized commitment, calls for the deepest embodiment of these principles. It requires a maturity that chooses kindness and patience as default settings, that practices non-violent communication even in frustration, and that offers support unconditionally. It involves protecting the partnership by not speaking ill of each other to outsiders, taking joint responsibility for life's management, and vigilantly avoiding corrosive dynamics like gaslighting or enmeshment. Crucially, it recognizes that each partner must steward their own happiness, bringing a full self to the union rather than a dependent half.

The common thread through all stages is the conscious setting aside of ego. It is the practice of vulnerability, of prioritizing empathy, especially when the other is hurt or confused, and of leading by example. The most powerful question one can ask is not "What can I get?" but "What can I contribute to this dynamic?" By focusing on becoming the partner you wish to have, cultivating kindness, patience, honesty, and thoughtfulness, you actively create the conditions for the relationship you want. This is the true power within your control: to use your own behavior to build a foundation of peace and love.

Notes for Chapter 11

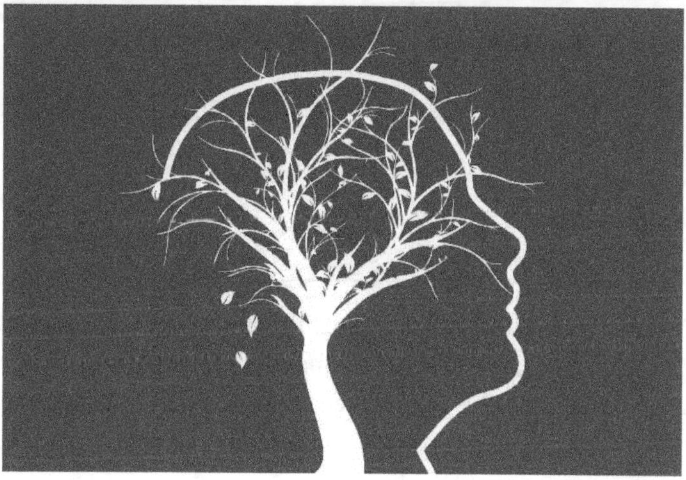

Key Takeaways

- **There are different kinds of romantic relationships, and each of them suits different groups of individuals, whether indefinitely or for a period of time.**
- **Every relationship has its own personality, and you need to navigate it as it goes. There's no one size that fits all.**
- **Similar to having different forms of relationships, there are distinct rules for maintaining each of these relationships.**
- **The things all romantic relationships have in common are vulnerability, constant empathy, putting your ego aside, leading by example, and putting your partner's happiness before yours during their difficult times. And most importantly, healthy communication!**

Chapter 12: How to Be Positive

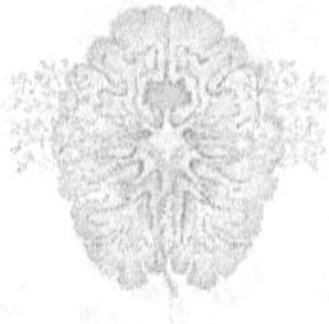

NOTE: Negative self-talk, hurtful language, and emotional pain can take many different forms. While this chapter cannot cover every possible experience, it is intended to address as much of the topic as possible and offer a meaningful place to begin.

Do you see your glass as half full or half empty? How you answer this classic question about positive thinking can reflect your outlook on life, your self-perception, whether you lean toward optimism or pessimism, and even the potential impact on your health. According to certain studies, temperamental qualities like pessimism and optimism can have an impact on a variety of aspects of your health and quality of life. Effective stress management relies heavily on the optimistic mindset that it typically entails. Additionally, effective stress management has a number of positive effects on health. You can develop positive thinking skills even if you have a tendency to be gloomy.

What Are Positive Thinking and Self-talk?

Positive thinking does not mean you should ignore less-than-ideal circumstances in life. Instead, positive thinking entails taking a constructive approach to bad situations. Instead of anticipating the worst, you expect the best outcome to happen.

The first step in positive thinking is usually self-talk also known as the continuous, never-ending flow of inner dialogue. Your self-talk is based on the flow of thoughts in your mind, some elements of logic, and reason. Thoughts, whether positive or negative may come to mind automatically. Sometimes, self-talk could result from assumptions made as a result of incomplete knowledge or anticipations brought on by preconceived notions of what might occur. Your general attitude toward life is much more likely to be negative if the majority of your thoughts are negative. Conversely, if your ideas are generally positive, you probably consider yourself an optimist or someone who engages in positive thinking.

How to Identify Positive or Negative Thinking?

Unsure if your inner dialogue is constructive or destructive? Typical examples of negative self-talk involve:

Filtering

You emphasize a situation's drawbacks while eliminating all of its advantages. For instance, your boss tells you that you are doing an amazing job and that you have been a great addition to the team. They are so lucky to have you, but they need you to dress just a bit more professionally. You go home, and when asked about your day, you only share that they want you to dress more professionally, leaving out all the compliments and how happy they are with you. An example of filtering, which we discussed in the topic of communication, is finding your personal filter for thinking before you speak. Mine, for example, is, "Is what I'm about to say going to hurt or help this person in front of me?" A filter for thoughts can be the same: "Is this thought helpful or hurtful?" Therefore, it should follow with, "Should you continue this thought or change it to one that's helpful to you?"

When my client, Ms. T., came to me for therapy, she was exhausted from a version of life that looked successful from the outside. The thirty-two-year-old marketing manager had recently received a promotion, was financially stable, and had close friends who cared about her. Yet none of that seemed to matter to her by the time she sat down in my office. What consumed her was a constant, punishing inner voice that left her feeling inadequate no matter what she achieved. "I know how this sounds," she said. "I know I should be grateful. But I can't hold onto anything good for more than a few minutes. If someone compliments me, I immediately assume they're just being polite. If I do well at work, I tell myself it was luck. If I make one mistake, that becomes the whole story."

She gave me an example from the week before. Her supervisor had praised her in front of the team for leading a difficult campaign. After the meeting, he had added one note about tightening the formatting on future presentations. By the time she got home, the praise had disappeared entirely from her mind.

"All I could hear was that I messed up the formatting," she said. "I barely even remembered the rest. I kept replaying it in my head. I thought, Of course. You fooled them for a while, but now they're seeing what you're actually like."

What she was describing was filtering in one of its clearest forms. Her mind was taking in the full picture, then discarding everything affirmative and clinging only to the one detail that confirmed her worst belief about herself.

"So what happened in that meeting?" I asked.

"I told you. I got criticized."

"Did you?"

She paused. "Well. Sort of."

"What else happened?"

She looked annoyed by the question at first, as though I were missing the obvious point. "He said I led the campaign well. He said the client specifically appreciated my work. He said I handled pressure well."

"And why did none of that count?"

Her eyes welled up before she answered. "Because it never feels true. The negative part feels true. The good part feels temporary."

That is often how destructive self-talk works. It does not simply offer commentary. It appoints itself judge and then treats every event as evidence for a prewritten verdict.

The work we did was not about forcing her into fake confidence or asking her to ignore constructive criticism. It was about helping her notice what her mind was doing in real time. I asked her to start writing down situations exactly as they occurred, divided into two columns: what happened, and what story she told herself about what happened.

A few weeks later, she brought in one of those entries.

"What happened," she read aloud, "my friend canceled dinner because her son was sick."

"And what story did you tell yourself?" I asked.

"That she was tired of me. That she didn't really want to see me. That people always pull away eventually."

We looked at each other for a moment.

"Do you see how fast that happened?" I asked.

She nodded slowly. "It's like my brain doesn't even ask for evidence. It just goes straight to the worst explanation."

Months into our work, she began catching herself sooner.

"I still have the first thought," she told me. "I still hear the old voice. But now there's a pause. Now I can say, That's not a fact. That's a fear."

That pause changed everything. She did not become someone who never doubted herself again. But she became someone less willing to let one negative thought erase an entire reality.

"I'm starting to understand something," she said one day. "My mind has not been telling me the truth. It's been telling me a familiar story. Those are not the same thing."

Personalizing

When anything awful happens, you immediately place the responsibility on yourself. For instance, when you learn that a night out with friends has been canceled, you assume that everyone didn't want to be near you.

When Ms. M. came to see me, she was not struggling with one crisis so much as a constant erosion of her sense of self. The twenty-eight-year-old graduate student described herself as "too sensitive for normal life," though it became clear very quickly that sensitivity was not the core issue. The issue was that she personalized nearly everything.

"If someone is quiet, I assume I've done something wrong," she said. "If a professor is brief in an email, I assume I disappointed them. If my roommate looks irritated, I start thinking through everything I said in the last twenty-four hours to figure out what I ruined."

That kind of thinking is exhausting because it makes the self the center of every negative shift in the room. It gives people a false sense of control while quietly convincing them they are at fault for things that were never theirs to carry.

She told me about a seminar presentation she had given a few days earlier. One classmate had seemed distracted and had not made eye contact afterward.

"I left feeling humiliated," she said. "I kept thinking, He must have thought I sounded stupid. Then I told myself everyone else probably noticed too and was just being nice."

"Did anyone actually say that?"

"No."

"Did anyone say anything else?"

She hesitated. "Two people said they liked my analysis. My professor said it was thoughtful."

"And that did not land?"

She gave a tired smile. "Not even a little."

Her mind had already chosen its interpretation. Once that happened, everything else was forced to orbit it.

There was sadness underneath this pattern, but also anger. She was tired of being derailed by other people's moods and expressions. She was tired of feeling responsible for feelings that did not belong to her.

So I asked her to consider something that made her visibly uncomfortable.

"What if not everything is about you?"

She laughed despite herself. "That sounds rude."

"I don't mean it rudely," I said. "I mean it as relief."

She got quiet then.

Relief is not always the first thing people associate with that idea, but it often is. If every silence is not about you, if every short reply is not rejection, if every distracted face is not evidence of your failure, then the world becomes less accusatory and more spacious.

We began practicing external explanations before internal blame. If someone seemed tense, she had to come up with six possibilities before landing on herself. Tired. Busy. Preoccupied. Grieving. Distracted. Human.

A month later, she came in with a story.

"My advisor sent me an email that just said, 'Please revise and resend.' No greeting, no smiley face, nothing. I immediately thought, She's irritated. She regrets taking me on. I'm difficult. Then I stopped. I made myself wait before spiraling."

"What happened next?"

"I revised the section and resent it. She replied two hours later, 'Much better, thank you.' That was it. She was just busy."

"And what did you learn?"

She leaned back in her chair. "That I have been volunteering for guilt nobody assigned to me."

That sentence stayed with me.

The deeper work that followed was about separating responsibility from reflex. She still cared deeply about how she affected other people. That was not the problem. The problem was that she had turned every ambiguous moment into an indictment of her worth.

Near the end of our work together, she told me, "I still have the instinct to assume I'm the problem. But now I catch it faster. I can tell the difference between actual accountability and old emotional habits."

That distinction changed her relationships. She became less apologetic, less frantic, and more present. She stopped trying to read everyone's mind and started listening to what was actually being said.

"Turns out," she said once with a small smile, "other people are allowed to have moods that have nothing to do with me."

Catastrophizing

Even in the absence of evidence, you instantly assume the worst will transpire. It can even be triggered by something insignificant. For example, if your order is misplaced at the drive-through coffeehouse, you may immediately fear that your entire day is going to go wrong.

Mr. F., a forty-four-year-old high school teacher, came to therapy after what he described as "a small thing that turned into a whole collapse." He had sent a text to his sister and did not hear back for most of the day. By evening, he was convinced she was angry with him, that he had said something wrong during their last conversation, and that yet another important relationship in his life was beginning to crack.

"She replied the next morning," he told me. "Her phone had died. That was it. Totally normal explanation. But by the time she texted back, I had already gone through every possible reason she might be done with me."

He laughed when he said it, but there was no humor in it. He looked embarrassed.

"This happens a lot," he admitted. "Something small happens, and within ten minutes I'm living in a disaster that doesn't even exist yet."

He described the way his thoughts escalated. A delayed email from his principal meant he was probably in trouble. A friend seeming distracted at lunch meant he had offended him. His daughter being quiet after school meant something was terribly wrong. His mind did not stay with uncertainty for long. It rushed past it into catastrophe.

Catastrophizing often masquerades as preparation. It convinces people that if they imagine the worst in advance, they will be safer when life goes wrong. In reality, it usually just means they suffer several times before anything has even happened.

"What do you think your mind is trying to do for you?" I asked.

"Protect me, maybe."

"By doing what?"

"By assuming disaster before it gets here."

"And does it help?"

He shook his head. "No. It ruins entire days. Sometimes whole weeks."

We traced the pattern back to earlier years. He had grown up in a house where bad news often arrived without warning.

A slammed door, a certain tone of voice, a silence that lasted too long, all of it meant something was coming. His mind had learned that scanning for danger was necessary. What had once been an adaptation had followed him into a life where it no longer fit the facts.

One afternoon, he came in after an especially difficult week. His principal had written, "Can we talk tomorrow?" with no further explanation.

"I barely slept," he said. "I assumed I was being reprimanded. I replayed every class. Every parent interaction. I thought maybe there had been a complaint. I was already mentally updating my résumé."

"And what did she want?"

He exhaled. "To ask if I would help mentor a new teacher."

We both sat there for a second.

"That's what this does to me," he said quietly. "I don't live in my actual life. I live in the disaster version of it."

So we practiced a structured interruption. When he noticed himself leaping to the worst-case scenario, he had to ask three questions: What do I know? What am I assuming? What is another possible explanation?

He resisted the exercise at first.

"It feels simplistic," he said.

"It is simple," I told him. "Simple is not the same as ineffective."

A few months later, he came in smiling.

"My daughter didn't answer her phone last weekend," he said. "I had the thought immediately. Car accident. Emergency. Something terrible. Then I stopped and asked the questions. What do I know? I know she didn't answer. What am I assuming? That something awful happened. What is another explanation? She's twenty, she left her phone in another room, and she's making pancakes with music on."

"And?"

"And that was exactly it."

He laughed then, but this time there was relief in it.

"I'm not suddenly cured," he said. "But I'm not worshipping every worst-case scenario anymore. I'm learning that uncertainty is uncomfortable, but it is not the same thing as danger."

Blaming

You try to deflect responsibility by putting the fault on someone else instead of owning your own thoughts and feelings.

Telling yourself you "should" take action

You make long mental lists of what you ought to do, then criticize yourself when you don't complete them.

Focusing on Positive Thinking

"A positive mind finds opportunity in everything. A negative mind finds fault in everything."

-B.K. Shivani

You can train your mind to replace negative thoughts with positive ones. While the process is simple, it takes consistency and patience, since you're building a new habit—and habits take time to develop. The following approaches can help you adopt a more positive and balanced mindset:

Identify what needs to change

If you want to become more optimistic, begin by noticing the areas of your life where your thoughts tend to turn negative—whether it's your work, commute, future goals, or relationships. Focus on one area at a time and approach it with a more constructive perspective. Instead of defaulting to negative thinking as a way to cope with stress, practice shifting toward more positive interpretations.

___

___

___

Assess yourself

Pause periodically throughout the day to assess your thoughts. Look for a way to reframe your ideas if you notice they are primarily negative.

Do you have one to practice on?

Allow yourself to be amused

Give yourself the freedom to laugh or grin, especially when things are tough. Find humor in commonplace events. You will feel lighter if you can laugh at life.

Let's give it a try.

Maintain a fit lifestyle

On the majority of days of the week, try to get in 30 minutes of exercise. During the day, you can also divide it into five or ten-minute intervals. Stress reduction and mood improvement are two benefits of exercise. Eat healthy and drink water to nourish both your body and mind. Get adequate rest and acquire stress management skills. List a goal to accomplish this.

Be in the company of uplifting individuals

Make sure the individuals you surround yourself with are upbeat, encouraging, and capable of providing insightful feedback. People who are negative-minded might make you feel more stressed out and make you question your capacity to handle stress in constructive ways.

Engage in constructive self-talk

Start by adhering to this straightforward principle: don't speak to yourself in a way you wouldn't speak to someone else. Be kind and supportive to yourself. When a negative thought arises, analyze it logically and counter it by focusing on your positive traits. Consider the aspects of your life for which you are grateful.

I have my own clients replace every negative self-talk with three positive ones.

Exercise:

Write three negative self-talk comments.

____

____

____

____

____

Now replace each of these with three positive self-talk comments. (or more if you'd like)

Practicing to Think Positive Everyday

Expecting to be an optimist overnight is unrealistic if you have a tendency to be pessimistic. But over time, you'll become less critical of yourself and more accepting of who you are. You can also start to lose your sense of self-criticism. As a perk, being less critical of oneself will result in you being less critical of others, too!

Having a generally positive outlook helps you manage daily stress more effectively. That aptitude could be a factor in the well-documented health advantages of positive thinking.

Remember, your brain has neuroplasticity (its lifelong capacity to change and rewrite itself in response to the stimulation of experiences and learning), so practice, the change will occur. You can achieve this! You got this!

What is Positive Language?

In everyday conversations, we often slip into negative language, using words like "don't," "not," "can't," and "won't." Over time, these expressions shape how we see ourselves, influence our outlook on life, and even guide our behavior—often without us realizing it, since this way of communicating has become habitual. Developing a positive way of speaking is a valuable skill, whether you're interacting with children, colleagues, or your own inner voice.

For the majority of people, spoken or written words serve as the primary means of interaction, whereas nonverbal cues like posture or emotional expression serve as supporting cues that help frame the message. Our intellect and thoughts are formed by the language we use, and vice versa.

Utilizing negative or positive language in daily conversation, as well as in self-talk, shapes the relationships we share with other individuals and has an impact on how we feel and perceive ourselves, which influences our behavior.

Positive language is educational, proactive, and beneficial in contrast to constrictive, unenlightening, and confining negative language. Positive language is a way of delivering a cheerful and encouraging tone to your communicators, whether they be customers, co-workers, kids, household members, or, obviously, oneself.

Why Use Positive Language?

Using positive language benefits people of all ages. Whether you are in a personal or professional setting, when you use positive language in your interactions, it spreads good messages and helps foster a cheerful outlook.

While positive language should be an integral part of all communications, people working in areas that involve customer assistance are usually more conscious of using positive words.

For instance, instead of telling a customer straight away, "I can't help you with this issue," they would say something like, "Let me connect you to somebody who can assist you with this problem in particular. Thank you, I appreciate your understanding and patience so much."

Do you see the difference? You don't have to start calling customer support to learn to communicate positively and affirmatively, so don't worry. I will give you a thorough explanation of positive language. I will provide you with several instances and discuss how they vary from negative scenarios.

Advantages of Positive Language

Improved Self-Image

Exercise: What words would you choose to define who you are? (Be raw and honest; what comes up naturally)

____

____

____

____

____

____

____

____

Rather than worrying about what you shouldn't or couldn't do, you should focus more on what you can do and achieve. Positive language works like positive affirmations, helping you boost your perspective of yourself.

When talking about yourself and describing your personality, try to use as many positive phrases as possible. The more positive phrases you use to express your personality and skills, the easier it becomes for you to embrace your flaws and view yourself as more compelling and motivating. This practice shifts your focus from your flaws to your positive traits and frees you from self-limiting ideas. As a result, you can release your maximum potential and realize what you really deserve.

A rigid perspective and the idea that there isn't much you can do to enhance your life and increase your skills are both components of negative language. It is centered on evading uncomfortable and unsettling situations rather than coping with them.

Positive language embraces the idea of a progressive mindset, a positive mindset, and the conviction that anything is achievable with enough effort and clear direction. And that's precisely what using positive language does for you: it inspires you and builds your character.

Exercise: Now, *using only positive phrases, define who you are.*

Improved Health and Temperament

Since our language influences our beliefs, and our beliefs influence our feelings, moving from unfavorable or moderate language to positive language can significantly affect our mood and overall health.

Positive language conveys a supportive, self-assured, and upbeat attitude, while negative language shows a bad attitude and temperament.

Without being aware of it, your temperament affects how people interact with you, further enforcing your positive or negative experiences, thoughts, and feelings, so why not choose a positive life, way, experience, and attitude?

A Role Model for Others

Adopting positive language in ordinary conversation can motivate those around you to be optimistic and put forth a lot of effort to realize their own goals. Positive language positions you as a leader in your community, and this kind of personality inspires others by serving as an example to them.

When you speak in a positive, upbeat, and affirmative manner, you not only establish a good mood and a welcoming environment but also keep others engaged and eager to assist.

Improved Office Environment

The nature of relationships between co-workers, the company's objective, the efficacy of teams, and the relationship between workers and supervisors can all greatly benefit from positive language in the office. Additionally, the language you use in a job interview can be extremely important in determining if you get the job since it conveys your objectives, passion, and desire to find a solution to a particular problem. Even if your skill set is fit for the job title, your language may show indecision, a dearth of ambition, and ambiguity. On the other side, speaking positively conveys tenacity, initiative, and confidence.

Improved Parent-Child Relationship

You are teaching your kids how to behave positively by using positive language. Children who are subjected to continual criticism and directives such as "Stop doing that," "You can't do this," "This is not how it's done," etc., become defensive, frustrated, and lose their independence and enthusiasm to experience the world on their own.

Contrarily, positive language motivates kids to take ownership of their actions, make responsible decisions on their own, and improve their self-esteem. Rather than concentrating on bad behaviors, it enables kids to concentrate on and learn from good ones.

Any problematic dialogue or circumstance may be improved with the correct verbal and written word choices and effective communication that stimulates and drives action. Positive language is about employing language that comforts, encourages, and offers options, not about avoiding negative or difficult issues or giving bad news with a false grin. Using positive language with kids also helps them to trust their gut instincts.

Pointers For Applying Positive Language

To rebuild your vocabulary, you'll have to be highly attentive and aware of the language you use every day. Start by refraining from using derogatory language and rephrasing common phrases like "No problem" and "I can't find it!" Eventually, as your brain gradually changes to become more optimistic, you'll begin speaking positively on the fly.

Although some aspects will require some practice, particularly your speaking, given its quick and occasionally spontaneous speed, here are a few basic ideas you can put into practice straight away:

- **Rephrase sentences that contain negative terms like "can' t," "won' t," "don' t," "stop," or "shouldn' t," as well as those that start with prefixes like "-un," "-in," or "-ir" (inopportune, unkind, inept, irresponsible, etc.).**
- **When stating that something cannot be done, provide a replacement rather than apologize. This**

advances the discussion and fosters a climate that is focused on finding solutions.

- **Even under challenging circumstances, have a grateful mindset and pay attention to the little things. When receiving unfavorable criticism (AKA constructive criticism) or experiencing a sense of stagnation, look for a chance to advance. This will assist you in maintaining a cheerful attitude and seeing things as opportunities for growth.**
- **Use gentle words; they help to reduce tension. The same is true for compliments, showing thanks, and asking others what they can do to improve a situation.**
- **Remain confident in your body language. When speaking, make an effort to smile and keep your body relaxed. When you' re feeling apprehensive, attempt some breathing techniques to relax, maintain a relaxed physique, and speak softly (or else, your interlocutor will feel tense and uneasy too).**

Effective communication involves using positive language. It not only makes you feel good, but also makes the recipient feel secure and motivated. It also promotes a positive inner dialogue and helps you feel at home anywhere. By supporting your goals and building lasting relationships rooted in respect and empathy, it creates a foundation for long-term success. Positive communication, according to Dr.

Julien C. Mirivel, PhD, a professor of Applied Communication, involves being deliberate.

"As a leader, a parent, a partner, or a friend, we can all choose to use our words to do a little good."

Exercise: Now that we've had the discussion, let's practice our positive talk again. Redundancy enables memories to persist over time as teams of neurons all fire in synchrony in stable memories. Let's describe you positively.

Write positive self-affirmations.

Rephrase some of your common negative phrases into positives.

____

____

____

____

____

____

____

How does positive thinking affect us on a cellular level?

Not only are you hanging your life, becoming the best version of yourself, but you are physically changing your brain, cellularly changing your energy vibrations. An all-around transformation! The mirage of yourself in the near future that you perceived when you first picked up this book isn't a mirage once you have done the work; it's your new reality, your new side, a happier you.

If you don't have enough reasons by now to practice the power of positive thought, I don't know how else to convince you.

Notes For Chapter 12

Key Takeaways

- **Be true to yourself. In the face of maliciousness, be the bigger person. Do it for you.**
- **Don't change who you are because of someone else mistreating you. Take the higher road; you'll feel better.**
- **Speak positively. Think positively to have a positive outlook on life and speak to others with respect. Understand how positive thinking and speaking can positively affect all of your relationships and your personal outlook on experiences.**
- **Filters: We should use filters throughout life. For example, my personal filter for speaking is, "Is what I'm about to say going to make the other person feel good right now or feel bad? If it will make the other person feel bad, is what I'm about to say necessary for change, or just hurtful?" The same applies to you. Reflect on whether what you're thinking or saying to yourself will hurt you or make you feel good.**
- **Replace every negative comment outwardly or self-talk inwardly with three positive comments every time you're aware of doing it.**

Chapter 13: The Energy That Makes You

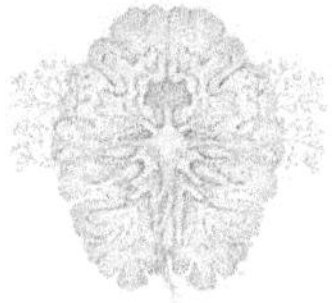

A perspective emerging in both complementary medicine and physics suggests we are more than just our physical mass; we are also dynamic systems of energy. At the most fundamental level, our bodies are composed of particles in constant motion, generating and emitting energy fields, however subtle.

This concept forms the basis of energy or vibrational medicine, which seeks to understand how these subtle energies influence health and well-being. While often viewed as spiritual, this idea intersects with established science: our bodies demonstrably produce electrical and magnetic activity that drives essential chemical processes, and research continues to explore how modulating these energies might affect health outcomes.

To understand this, we must consider vibration. Vibration is a rhythmic oscillation, a pattern of movement. We witness it on a grand scale in the cycles of seasons and tides. We witness it within ourselves in the palpable rhythms of our heartbeat, our breath, and our circadian sleep-wake cycle.

These observable rhythms are the macro expression of a microscopic reality. Within each of our cells, molecules vibrate at specific frequencies, movements so infinitesimally small they are beyond physical sight. These vibrations generate subtle electromagnetic energy waves. The central theory posits that the quality, balance, and rate of these vibrations can influence cellular function and, by extension, our overall state.

These vibrational rates are not static. They are influenced by their environment. Just as temperature can change a molecule's speed of vibration, our internal and external conditions, from our emotional state to the quality of our thoughts, are theorized to potentially affect this delicate energetic symphony.

How do our thoughts and behaviors affect these vibrations?

Research confirms that our thoughts and behaviors directly influence our body's observable rhythms. Anxiety triggers stress hormones that accelerate the heart; calming music can slow breathing and shift mood. Building on this, some vibrational energy theorists propose a deeper hypothesis: that our mental and emotional patterns might also influence the subtlest vibrational rhythms at the cellular level. The idea is that by consciously shifting our thoughts and behaviors, we might positively affect these foundational vibrations, which could, in turn, promote better mental and physical health.

While the precise mechanics of how subtle energy translates to well-being remain a frontier of science, the proposed benefits align with well-documented mind-body principles. Proponents suggest that harmonizing the body's vibrations may help regulate mood, support physical health, and foster a mental state conducive to achieving personal goals.

Central to this theory is the concept of vibrational frequency. It is proposed that positive emotional states, such as joy, peace, and acceptance, are associated with higher, more coherent frequencies. In contrast, chronic negative states like fear, anger, and despair are linked with lower, more disordered frequencies.

Regardless of one's stance on vibrational mechanics, the underlying principle is supported by considerable evidence: cultivating positive emotions and constructive thought patterns is irrefutably linked to improved health outcomes, greater resilience, and a higher likelihood of personal fulfillment. The language of vibration, therefore, can serve as a valuable metaphor for the tangible, life-enhancing power of a positive inner state.

Ways to Change One's Vibrational Energy

While science continues to explore the mechanisms, many traditions and holistic practices aim to harmonize the mind-body system, which can be usefully framed as cultivating a balanced, positive energy state. These practices share a common thread: they pull us out of reactive, stressful patterns and into a state of greater coherence and presence.

Breath work is a foundational tool. Rhythmic, controlled breathing directly calms the nervous system, slows the heart rate, and activates brain regions associated with emotional regulation. It is a direct method to shift your physiological and emotional state toward calm.

Meditation trains mindful observation, creating a quiet mental space separate from your reactions. Regular practice is shown to reduce activity in the brain's stress centers, leading to tangible benefits like lowered blood pressure, reduced pain sensitivity, and alleviated symptoms of anxiety and insomnia.

Cultivating gratitude consciously redirects attention toward positivity. This practice enhances psychological well-being, reduces stress, and makes you more likely to engage in other health-promoting behaviors, effectively raising your overall resilience.

Acts of generosity and prosocial behavior not only benefit others but also generate intrinsic rewards, reducing the harmful physiological impacts of chronic stress and contributing to a sense of purpose and connection.

Diet and environment play crucial roles in our baseline energy. Nourishing your body with whole, unprocessed foods provides the clean fuel necessary for optimal function.

Similarly, immersion in nature, exposure to natural light, sound, and air has a demonstrable, calming effect on the nervous system, lowering stress hormones and improving vital signs.

Practices like yoga integrate breath, movement, and meditation, offering exceptional benefits for both cognitive and physical health, from improved brain connectivity to better cardiovascular function.

Finally, healthy relationships are perhaps the most powerful modulator of our ongoing emotional and energetic state. Supportive social connections provide a buffer against stress, enrich life with meaning, and are strongly correlated with longevity and health.[13]

Whether interpreted literally or metaphorically, the principle is sound: our thoughts, behaviors, and interactions create a continuous feedback loop within our biology. By consciously engaging in practices that foster internal harmony, we construct a life where our mental, emotional, and physical aspects are more likely to work in integrated alignment.

Science of the Heart

For millennia, the heart has been symbolically linked to emotion and wisdom. Modern science has now revealed a

---

[13] Three Initiates. (1908). The Kybalion: A study of the Hermetic philosophy of ancient Egypt and Greece. Yogi Publication Society.

literal, complex dialogue between the heart and the brain, challenging the old paradigm of the brain as sole commander. This communication is a dynamic, two-way street where each organ profoundly influences the other. According to researchers at HeartMath Institute (n.d.), the heart communicates with the brain through several parallel pathways: neurological signals via the nervous system, biochemical messages via hormones, biophysical information through pulse waves, and energetic interactions via electromagnetic fields.[14]

The heart possesses its own intricate nervous system, often called the "heart-brain," which is sophisticated enough to operate independently. This discovery gave rise to the field of neurocardiology. Intriguingly, the heart sends more signals to the brain than it receives. These signals influence key brain centers involved in perception, cognition, and emotional processing.

Beyond its neurological role, the heart functions as a hormonal gland. In the 1980s, science reclassified it as part of the endocrine system after discovering it produces atrial natriuretic peptide, a hormone crucial for fluid balance that also helps reduce stress hormones and calm the nervous system.

---

[14] HeartMath Institute. (n.d.). Heart–brain communication. https://www.heartmath.org

Further research revealed the heart also synthesizes neurotransmitters, including norepinephrine, dopamine, and oxytocin, the so-called "love hormone" integral to bonding, trust, and social connection. The heart produces oxytocin in concentrations comparable to the brain.

These findings fundamentally expand our understanding. The heart is not merely a pump responsive to the brain's commands; it is a central player in a continuous, intelligent feedback loop that governs our physical health, shapes our emotional experience, and underpins our mental well-being.

Ms. Q., a forty-two-year-old emergency dispatcher who came to therapy, explained that she had been experiencing panic attacks that made no logical sense.

Upon further inquiry, she told me that she would often be sitting at her desk, completely calm, handling a routine call, and suddenly her heart would start racing. I asked if she had consulted a cardiologist, and she told me that she had, in fact, been to three cardiologists who had run every test.

"My heart is structurally perfect. They all say the same thing: it is anxiety. But I am not anxious. I am fine. And then my heart starts pounding for no reason and convinces my brain that something is wrong."

This was a precise reversal of the usual narrative. Most people experience anxiety as a mental state that produces physical symptoms. Ms. Q. was experiencing physical activation that her brain then interpreted as danger.

I asked her to describe what happens right before her heart starts racing.

She thought carefully and then told me that she would feel nothing. "One second I am fine, the next my heart is pounding."

We began training something she had never practiced: interoception, the ability to perceive internal bodily states. I taught her to do body scans throughout her shift to notice her heart rate, her breath, the tension in her shoulders, and the temperature of her hands.

Three weeks later, she came back with the discovery that her chest tightened right before her heart started racing.

"And what is happening when your chest gets tight?"

She pulled out a log she had been keeping. "A caller is screaming. Or a call involves a child. Or someone is describing an injury in graphic detail. The content is distressing, but I am trained to stay calm and get the information I need. I do not feel anxious. I do my job. But my chest tightens, and then thirty seconds later, my heart starts racing."

This was the heart-brain dialogue in action. Her heart was responding to distress before her conscious mind registered it. The heart's electromagnetic field and neural signals were communicating stress to her brain, which then amplified the response into what felt like a panic attack.

"Your heart is not malfunctioning," I told her. "It is perceiving a threat in the content you are hearing and trying to alert you. Your brain has learned to dismiss emotional responses as unprofessional, so it does not register the initial signal. But your heart keeps trying to tell you, and eventually it has to scream loudly enough, through racing, that your brain finally pays attention."

We worked on acknowledging the heart's signals early rather than waiting for them to escalate. When she felt chest tightness, rather than pushing through it, she would take three slow breaths, place her hand over her heart, and mentally acknowledge that feeling those emotions was being human.

The panic attacks did not disappear immediately. But they decreased. More importantly, she began to perceive them as communication from her heart that she had been trained to ignore until it became impossible to dismiss.

Energy In Motion

We have explored the impact of emotions, but to understand their power, we must examine their mechanics. Emotions are not merely mental events; they are felt as distinct physical sensations within the body. The rhythm of your breath, the tension in your muscles, the flutter in your stomach, each emotion carries a unique energetic signature that directly alters your physiological state.

This is because emotions are, in essence, forms of energy moving through our biology. Happiness, anger, sadness, and anxiety each produce specific waves of sensation and temperature change. This energy directly influences how we think, act, and perceive our physical well-being.

Attempting to suppress or avoid these feelings disrupts the body's natural processing mechanism. When the energy of an emotion is blocked from moving through and being released, it does not simply vanish. It can become stored, creating a buildup of unresolved intensity. Over time, this reservoir of trapped emotional energy can manifest in various detrimental ways, such as heightened anxiety, addictive behaviors, perfectionistic striving, or chronic self-criticism.

This stagnation lowers our overall vitality, negatively impacting both mental and physical health. The path forward is not to fight the emotion, but to first acknowledge its presence and the challenge it represents. From that place of acknowledgment, you can consciously apply the harmonizing practices discussed earlier, mindful breath, meditation, gratitude, and physical expression to gently release the stored energy, clear the stagnation, and restore a natural, healthier flow within your mind and body.

Notes for Chapter 13

Key Takeaways

- **Our bodies produce vibrational energy**
- **These vibrations are like rhythms, which are very tiny, similar to nano organisms present in our body**
- **These vibrations create electromagnetic waves in our bodies**
- **This energy, affected by our behavior and thoughts, shapes our emotional and physical health, changing the pace at which it produces vibrations**
- **However, by getting involved in positive and healthy activities, we can improve the rate of these vibrations**
- **Our hearts and minds are connected, engaged in two-way, dynamic communication**
- **Emotions are forms of energy that move throughout our bodies**
- **This energy keeps changing according to the situation we experience**
- **This change of energy is evident in the physical changes we undergo, like changes in temperature or breathing patterns**

Chapter 14: Integration Under Pressure

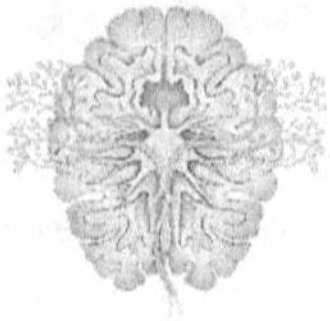

At this stage in your journey, change should no longer feel mystical or subtle. If the work in this book has been applied honestly, it will have created friction. Awareness does not arrive quietly; it interrupts habits, exposes inconsistencies, and forces you to confront where your actions do not match your values. If nothing feels uncomfortable, nothing has truly shifted. This chapter is not about acquiring new insight. It is about accountability: the point where understanding meets behavior.

Integration is where understanding becomes behavior. It is not how clearly you can describe your emotions, but how consistently you respond when they arise. It is not what you know about your patterns, but whether those patterns still control you. Integration is measurable. It shows up in the pause you take before reacting, the boundary you hold even when it costs you approval, and the choices you make when no one is watching.

Growth does not fail from lack of insight. It fails because insight is seldom practiced under pressure. When stress increases, the nervous system defaults to what is familiar, not what is learned. This is why intellectual understanding alone is fragile. It collapses in moments of fear, conflict, or exhaustion. What survives stress is what has been practiced repeatedly and deliberately. Becoming the mirror means one thing: you stop outsourcing self-recognition. You no longer rely on crisis, feedback, or conflict to reveal who you are. You observe yourself in real time. You notice when your body tightens, when your thoughts accelerate, when old narratives attempt to reassert control. And instead of being pulled into them, you stay present enough to choose differently. This is not a poetic idea. It is a discipline.

There will be moments when integration feels like loss. You may release relationships that depended on your compliance. You may lose identities built on struggle, chaos, or over-functioning. You may even lose the comfort of blaming circumstances or other people for your inner state. This discomfort is not evidence of failure; it is evidence of transition.

Continuity prevents regression. It is the willingness to return to yourself again and again, even after setbacks. Integration does not mean you no longer fall back into old habits; it means you recognize it faster and stay there for less time. Progress is not linear. It is recursive.

Earlier in this book, the mirror was a tool for self-examination. Now it becomes a standard. To become the mirror is to reflect truth without distortion or self-deception. It is to see yourself clearly enough that excuses lose their power. This is where the work becomes yours alone. No chapter can do this for you. No insight can replace practice. From here forward, growth is sustained not by reading but by repetition, restraint, and responsibility. You are no longer learning who you are. You are learning to live as if you already know.

From Awareness to Integration

The earlier chapters trained you to observe yourself with precision. You learned to notice habits without justifying them, to identify emotional patterns without dramatizing them, and to name values without turning them into slogans. Awareness created distance. Distance made choice possible. But awareness, on its own, is unstable. It sharpens perception without guaranteeing change.

Integration is the narrowing of that gap. Integration is not insight. It is not emotional vocabulary. It is not the ability to explain yourself convincingly. Integration is the consistent translation of awareness into behavior under ordinary and stressful conditions alike. It is the difference between recognizing a pattern and interrupting it in real time. This is where many people stall. Awareness feels productive, even virtuous. Integration can even feel too costly.

To integrate is to act differently when the old response would be easier, faster, or socially rewarded. It means responding instead of reacting, not because you are calm, but because you have trained yourself to tolerate discomfort without immediately discharging it. It means setting boundaries not when you feel confident, but when you feel afraid of being misunderstood or rejected. It means validating your own experience before seeking confirmation from others, even when silence makes you uneasy.

Integration can be observed. It shows up in specific, repeatable behaviors: You notice an emotional trigger as it emerges, not after it has already dictated your response. You pause long enough to choose a behavior aligned with your values, even when your nervous system urges speed or defense. You accept the relational or emotional cost of that choice without rushing to repair the discomfort. This is not moral superiority. It is a nervous system discipline.

Congruence—the alignment between inner experience and outward action—is often misunderstood as harmony. In practice, congruence frequently feels like tension. When your internal clarity exceeds your external habits, discomfort is inevitable. Old strategies resist replacement. Relationships renegotiate their terms. Identities that relied on inconsistency begin to collapse.

This friction is not a sign that integration is failing. It is the mechanism by which it works. Congruence is achieved not when conflict disappears, but when your actions remain intelligible to you even in conflict. You may still feel anger, fear, or doubt. What changes is that these states no longer dictate behavior by default. You remain responsible for your responses, regardless of how justified your emotions feel.

Integration also demands repetition. One aligned choice does not establish congruence. Patterns change through frequency, not intensity. The work is quiet and often unremarkable: choosing restraint again, holding a boundary again, returning to self-observation again. Progress is measured not by the absence of regression, but by reduced duration and faster recovery when regression occurs.

Awareness opened the door. Integration requires walking through it repeatedly, deliberately, and without guarantees. This is the point where self-understanding becomes self-governance. Not perfection. Not emotional purity. Congruence.

One of my clients was Dr. S., a forty-seven-year-old psychologist who had been in therapy with me for two years. She was frustrated about the lack of action on her awareness.

"I know exactly what I am doing," she said. "I can identify the pattern as it is happening. I can feel myself about to people-please, about to soften a boundary I set, about to agree to something that violates my stated limits. I see it. I understand it. I can explain the childhood roots, the relational dynamics, and the cost to my well-being. And then I do it anyway."

This is the particular torment of the highly self-aware: knowledge without power, insight without integration. Dr. S.

had done exceptional therapeutic work. She could articulate her patterns with clinical precision. She understood her triggers, her avoidance strategies, her core wounds. She had awareness that most people never achieve. And she was still saying yes when she meant no. Still taking on clients she did not have the capacity for. Still managing her partner's emotions instead of her own. Still apologizing for boundaries she had every right to set.

We often believe that awareness is the solution to our problems. We think that if we understand why we do something, we could stop doing it. But oftentimes, we end up doing the same thing, just with more self-awareness, which somehow makes it worse.

"Awareness is not the same as capacity," I told Dr. S. "You can see the pattern forming, but you cannot get rid of it until you have the nervous system tolerance to withstand the discomfort of choosing differently.

We spent the next six months building what I called "distress tolerance in the moment of choice." The moment when she could feel herself about to say yes despite wanting to say no was a moment for sitting in acute discomfort without immediately resolving it.

After six months, she told me how a colleague of hers had asked her to take on an additional administrative task the previous week, reviewing case study notes ahead of a multidisciplinary meeting. She quickly identified that she did not have the capacity. While she could feel the yes forming in her mouth like a reflex, she made herself wait. "I said, 'Let me check my schedule and get back to you.' I left the room. I sat in my office and felt like I was going to crawl out of my skin with discomfort. The urge to text her immediately and say yes was overwhelming. I wanted to relieve the tension. But I made myself sit with it for thirty minutes."

"And then?" I asked.

"I texted her: 'I cannot this week.' And then I had a panic attack because I had said no to someone who needed help."

"That panic is your nervous system realizing you broke a survival pattern it has relied on for forty-seven years," I said. " You just demonstrated that you can tolerate disapproval and still survive. That is new information for your body."

"Integration is not about never feeling the pull to people-please," I told her. "It is about narrowing the gap between noticing the pull and choosing something different. Right now, that gap is thirty minutes. Eventually, it might be thirty seconds. But there will always be a gap, and there will always be discomfort in that gap. Integration is the willingness to stay in the gap long enough to choose."

A year later, she was able to say no and create boundaries without needing to self-isolate to regulate herself. She still felt a little guilty, but she stood by her decision.

Awareness tells you what you are doing and why. But integration teaches you that you can survive doing something different. Those are not the same thing. And it is important to understand the difference between the two.

The Illusion of "Arrival"

One of the most persistent myths in self-development is the expectation of completion. It is the belief that sufficient insight, healing, or effort will eventually produce a stable psychological state, one in which confidence is uninterrupted, emotional regulation is effortless, and old insecurities no longer resurface. This belief is not merely inaccurate; it is actively destabilizing.

There is no arrival point at which self-governance becomes automatic. What exists instead is a continuous process of regulation, recalibration, and return. Psychological stability is not a permanent achievement but a maintained condition. It degrades when unattended, much like physical strength or cognitive sharpness. The expectation of arrival encourages passivity. It suggests that one day the work will be done, and vigilance will no longer be necessary. In practice, this assumption is responsible for most regressions.

Even highly self-aware individuals experience fear, doubt, grief, and emotional reactivity. Awareness does not eliminate these states; it alters how quickly they are detected and how much authority they are given. The difference is not emotional purity, but response latency. Integration shortens the distance between activation and choice.

The illusion of arrival often reveals itself most clearly under stress. In periods of conflict, loss, fatigue, or rapid change, people discover that the emotional patterns they believed were resolved have merely been dormant. This is not evidence of failure. It is evidence that those patterns were suppressed by favorable conditions rather than restructured through practice.

The cost of believing in arrival is misplaced self-judgment. When discomfort reappears, the individual assumes something has gone wrong: that they have regressed, failed, or undone their progress. In reality, discomfort is not a diagnostic error. It is a signal demanding regulation rather than interpretation.

The work, then, is not the elimination of discomfort, but the refinement of one's response to it. Meeting discomfort differently requires restraint. It requires resisting the impulse to immediately explain, fix, externalize, or anesthetize what is being felt. It involves staying oriented to values when the nervous system is demanding relief. This is not intuitive. It must be trained.

Maintenance is not glamorous. It consists of repeated, deliberate acts: returning to self-observation, reestablishing boundaries, recalibrating expectations, and restoring congruence after disruption. Return is the defining skill, not avoidance, and not control.

Recalibration becomes necessary whenever circumstances change. New roles, deeper relationships, increased responsibility, and higher stakes will all expose limitations in previously sufficient strategies. Integration does not immunize you against this exposure; it equips you to respond without disintegration.

The illusion of arrival is attractive because it promises rest without responsibility. But psychological maturity does not remove effort; it directs it. The question is no longer whether discomfort will arise, but whether you will recognize it early enough to respond with intention.

You are not here to achieve a permanent internal state. You are here to maintain coherence under changing conditions.

And coherence is not sustained by insight alone, but by continuous, conscious return to what you already know how to do. As the rabbinic tradition reminds us: The work is not yours to finish, yet you are not free to desist from it. Obligation, not completion, is the point.

Mrs. V., a sixty-one-year-old woman who had completed intensive therapy five years earlier for complex PTSD, returned to see me. She told me she had been feeling a devastating disappointment in herself.

"I thought I was done," she said, tears already forming. "I did the work. Years of it. I processed the trauma. I learned to regulate. I built healthy relationships. I was confident, stable, present. I thought I had arrived at some permanent state of health. And then my daughter got engaged."

She described what had happened. Her daughter's fiancé came from a wealthy, socially prominent family. The wedding planning had become increasingly elaborate and formal. Her daughter's future mother-in-law had strong opinions about every detail and expected deference.

"And I froze," Mrs. V. said. "I reverted completely. Suddenly, I was the powerless, fawning version of myself I thought I had left behind. I could not advocate for my daughter. I could not set boundaries with this woman. I just smiled and agreed and felt myself shrinking smaller and smaller. All the progress I made—gone. Five years of therapy, wasted."

"Or," I said carefully, "five years of therapy encountering conditions you had never been tested under."

Her original trauma had involved a domineering, status-conscious mother who had used shame and social pressure to control her. In therapy, she had done profound work healing that wound, learning to set boundaries, and building self-worth independent of others' approval.

But she had never encountered someone who so precisely activated that old template while holding power over something she cared about deeply—her daughter's happiness and this significant family milestone.

"You did not undo five years of work," I told her. "You discovered that the work was not complete because the conditions that would truly test it had not yet arrived. This is not regression. This is the next layer."

We spent several sessions distinguishing between two types of pattern repetition. The first is true regression: returning to old behaviors when nothing has changed except your commitment. The second is encountering familiar patterns under genuinely novel, higher-stakes conditions. The first indicates backsliding. The second indicates that growth has reached a new edge.

"When you worked on boundaries with your mother, the stakes were your own well-being," I said. "Now the stakes include your daughter's wedding, her relationship with her in-laws, and family dynamics that will affect her for decades. Your nervous system is not stupid—it knows these are different stakes. The fawning response is not proof that you learned nothing. It is proof that you have encountered a scenario that requires integration at a level you have not yet practiced."

The work that followed was not about relearning basics. It was about applying established skills under conditions that made them far more costly. Learning to set boundaries with her future daughter-in-law-to-be, knowing it might create lasting family tension. Finding her voice in wedding planning without dominating or disappearing. Tolerating her daughter's occasional frustration when Mrs. V. could not simply make everything smooth.

"I keep expecting there to be a point where this gets easy," she said several months in. "Where I just automatically respond well to everything because I have done enough therapy."

"There is no automatic," I said. "There is only practiced. And sometimes you will encounter situations you have not practiced for yet. That does not mean you have failed. It means you are continuing to grow in increasingly complex circumstances. The measure of your five years of work is not that you did not freeze when tested. The measure is how quickly you recognized you were frozen and how willing you were to return and address it rather than staying frozen or pretending you were fine."

In our final session on this issue, she said, "I think I had this fantasy that therapy was like solving a math problem. Once you get the answer, you are done. But it is more like physical fitness. You can get very fit, but if you stop practicing or you attempt something more demanding than you have trained for, you will struggle. That does not mean you lost your fitness. It means you need to train at the new level."

She smiled, sad but genuine. "I am sixty-one years old. I thought by now I would have myself figured out. Instead, I am learning that every new life stage, every new relationship, every new challenge is going to ask me to grow in ways I have not yet grown. There is no arrival. There is only continued practice at higher and higher stakes."

The Mirror as a Practice

Earlier, the mirror functioned as an instrument of recognition. It allowed you to see patterns that operated unchecked, to identify emotional reflexes, habitual distortions, and the narratives you used to protect them. In this final stage, the mirror can no longer remain a passive surface. It must become an active practice. A practice implies repetition, resistance, and consequence.

The mirror is no longer a space for interpretation. It is a checkpoint. Its purpose is not self-analysis, reassurance, or critique, but verification. You do not approach it to understand yourself better, but to confirm whether your behavior remains aligned with what you already understand. The question it asks is not why, but whether alignment can be tested. The mirror, used correctly, reveals discrepancies between intention and action that are easy to overlook in motion. It exposes the quiet compromises: the boundary you softened to avoid tension, the reaction you justified as honesty, the value you deferred for convenience. These discrepancies are rarely dramatic. That is precisely why they accumulate.

This practice is intentionally limited. It is not performed daily, and it is not performed emotionally. Frequency dulls attention. Emotion invites distortion. The mirror is engaged deliberately, during periods of relative calm, when defensiveness is low, and perception is clear. Its function is calibration, not confession.

When you stand before the mirror, you are not there to recount feelings. You are there to assess behavior. The assessment is narrow and specific:

1. Where did my actions contradict my stated values this week?
2. Where did I respond automatically rather than deliberately?
3. Where did I notice discomfort and move away from it instead of regulating it?
4. Where did I maintain congruence despite internal resistance?

Each question demands an answer grounded in observable behavior, not interpretation. If an answer cannot be tied to a specific action, it is incomplete. The mirror also requires restraint. There is no correction at this moment. No promises. No self-instruction. The purpose is exposure, not repair. Repair occurs later, in context, through choice. Attempting to fix everything at once collapses the practice into self-management rather than self-governance.

The cost of this practice is honesty without immediacy. You will see misalignment and be required to tolerate it temporarily. This discomfort is deliberate. It strengthens your capacity to remain present with inconsistency rather than rushing to resolve it prematurely. Over time, this tolerance reduces the gap between recognition and response.

Continuity is sustained through return. You will miss things. You will rationalize. You will revert under pressure. The mirror is not a mechanism for punishment, but for reorientation. Each return reinforces the central skill: noticing deviation early enough to correct course before it becomes identity.

Used this way, the mirror ceases to be symbolic. It becomes operational. It does not tell you who you are. It tells you whether you are behaving in accordance with who you claim to be. This is the difference between reflection and regulation.

And regulation, practiced consistently, is what allows integration to endure.

Mirror Integration Exercise: Alignment Audit

Stand in front of a mirror in a quiet, neutral setting. Do not regulate your emotions beforehand. No breathing exercises, no grounding rituals. Discomfort is part of the practice.

Look at your reflection directly. Keep your posture neutral.

Ask the following questions out loud, and answer them factually, not emotionally:

In the past seven days, where did my actions contradict my stated values?

Name at least one specific situation and the behavior that followed.

Where did I notice discomfort and choose avoidance instead of regulation?

Identify what you avoided and how you avoided it.

When did I react automatically rather than respond deliberately?

Describe the trigger and your immediate response without justification.

Where did I maintain congruence despite internal resistance?

Identify one instance where alignment required effort.

What pattern is repeating that I am no longer justified in calling situational?

Name the pattern plainly.

Do not explain.

Do not defend.

Do not correct.

When you have answered, remain silent for thirty seconds. Maintain eye contact with your reflection. Notice any urge to rationalize, minimize, or promise change. Do nothing with it.

Now write your responses exactly as stated—short, concrete sentences only. Avoid all interpretation and emotional language and complete the exercise without planning next steps.

Behavioral correction will occur later, in context, through your actual choices. The purpose of this exercise is not insight or relief. It is verification.

Return to it only when enough time has passed for behavior to speak louder than intention.

Living in Alignment

Alignment is often mistaken for expression. In practice, it is a regulation. It is not the visible declaration of values, but the quiet enforcement of them under conditions that test resolve. Most aligned decisions are unremarkable to others and inconvenient to the person making them. That is precisely why they matter.

Alignment does not announce itself. It accumulates. It appears that the moment you decline an opportunity, it is not because it is harmful, but because it would require you to abandon a boundary you have already defined. It appears when you remain silent long enough to respond deliberately rather than securing relief through reaction. It appears when you choose rest without defending it, not as an act of indulgence, but as a refusal to override limits you already understand.

These decisions are not dramatic. They are repetitive. And they are costly. Living in alignment frequently disrupts existing arrangements. People who benefited from your inconsistency may resist your steadiness. Roles that relied on your availability may become unsustainable. The loneliness that often follows alignment is not incidental; it is structural. Congruence changes the terms of participation, and not all systems survive that change. This is where many people abandon alignment in favor of comfort. The pressure to maintain familiarity can feel more urgent than the long-term cost of self-betrayal. Alignment requires tolerating short-term isolation without rushing to resolve it. It demands restraint: the ability to remain in discomfort without renegotiating your values to regain approval.

Alignment also exposes internal contradictions. You may discover that some values were adopted aspirationally rather than embodied. When behavior repeatedly resists a stated value, the task is not increased force but reassessment. Living in alignment sometimes means revising what you claim to prioritize rather than forcing yourself into coherence prematurely.

Self-trust does not emerge from confidence. It emerges from predictability. When your actions consistently reflect your stated commitments, your nervous system learns that you are reliable. This reliability reduces internal negotiation. Decisions require less deliberation because precedent exists.

As self-trust increases, anxiety changes form. It does not disappear, but it loses its authority. Anxiety thrives in environments where behavior is inconsistent and outcomes are uncertain. Alignment reduces this volatility. When you know how you will act under pressure, fewer scenarios require rehearsal. Mental energy is conserved. Alignment is sustained through maintenance. Each aligned choice reinforces the next, but lapses are inevitable. The metric is not purity, but recovery time. How quickly do you notice deviation? How willingly do you correct course without self-punishment? These questions determine durability.

Living in alignment is not a personal branding exercise. It does not make life easier in the short term, nor does it guarantee relational harmony. What it produces is coherence. Coherence allows effort to be directed rather than diffused. It allows relationships to be negotiated honestly. It allows internal conflict to be resolved through action rather than rumination.

Alignment is not who you say you are. It is the pattern your behavior forms over time. And that pattern, once established, becomes the foundation upon which integration holds.

The Responsibility of Self-Knowledge

Self-knowledge is often presented as empowerment. In reality, it is liability before it is leverage. Once a pattern is seen clearly, it can no longer be treated as accidental. Awareness removes plausible deniability. What was once unconscious behavior becomes a choice by default if it continues unchanged. This is the point at which self-development becomes uncomfortable.

You begin to notice when you are self-betraying—not dramatically, but incrementally. You see the moment when you soften a boundary you had already identified, when you agree to something that contradicts your stated limits, when you remain silent to preserve ease rather than coherence. These moments are not catastrophic. Their danger lies in repetition. You also recognize people-pleasing not as kindness, but as a regulatory strategy. It becomes evident when approval is sought to stabilize internal discomfort rather than to build connection. What once felt like generosity reveals itself as avoidance—of conflict, of rejection, of responsibility for your own stance.

Fear, too, becomes more difficult to disguise. With self-knowledge, fear no longer presents itself as emotion alone. It often masquerades as logic, timing, or restraint. You recognize the internal arguments that delay action under the guise of prudence. Awareness does not silence these arguments; it exposes their function. This exposure carries weight. Self-knowledge demands response.

The common reassurance that awareness is meant to free you is incomplete. It frees you from confusion, but it binds you to responsibility. You are no longer entitled to act as if you did not see the pattern forming. You cannot unknow the cost of certain behaviors, nor can you claim surprise when outcomes repeat.

Freedom, in this context, is frequently misunderstood. It does not mean the absence of constraint. It means the capacity to choose deliberately in the presence of constraint. Freedom is exercised when you act in alignment with what you know, despite internal resistance or external pressure.

This responsibility is cumulative. Each time you notice a misalignment and choose not to address it, the cost increases. The gap between knowledge and behavior widens, and with it comes internal friction—experienced as restlessness, anxiety, or erosion of self-trust. These are not symptoms to be managed; they are signals of deferred responsibility.

Conversely, choosing in accordance with self-knowledge reinforces coherence. Even when the choice is difficult or unpopular, it restores internal order. The nervous system responds to predictability. When your actions consistently reflect what you understand to be true, internal negotiation decreases.

Self-knowledge does not require constant action. It requires timely action. Not every insight demands immediate correction, but every recurring pattern demands eventual response. Delay is not neutral; it is a decision with consequences.

This is why self-knowledge cannot be treated as an internal achievement. It is not something you possess. It is something you are accountable for. The question is no longer whether you understand yourself, but whether you are willing to live in accordance with that understanding. Responsibility is the price of clarity. And clarity, once earned, does not permit retreat.

Continuing the Work

This book does not mark an ending. It establishes a standard. *What follows is not exploration, but application.* The work now shifts away from reflection and toward

maintenance, often unnoticed, frequently unacknowledged, and rarely affirmed by others.

Most of the work will occur outside moments of insight.

It happens in conversations you delay because they introduce tension, yet ultimately clarify terms. It happens in boundaries enforced without explanation, justification, or emotional performance. It happens in the restraint that you practice when reacting would feel more satisfying than responding. These moments do not announce themselves as growth. They register later, as coherence.

Continuing the work requires a recalibration of expectations. Progress will no longer feel expansive. Early awareness creates momentum because discovery is stimulating. Integration, by contrast, is repetitive. It requires revisiting the same principles under slightly different conditions, with marginally improved response times. This is not stagnation. It is a consolidation. Growth is cyclical, but not circular. You will encounter familiar patterns again, but with altered context and increased responsibility. What once required recognition now requires regulation. What once demanded compassion now demands correction. Revisiting a lesson does not indicate failure; it indicates that the stakes have increased.

Outgrowing earlier versions of yourself often feels like a loss. Strategies that once ensured survival may become inefficient or counterproductive. Identities built around struggle, intensity, or accommodation may no longer fit. Letting go of them can produce uncertainty rather than relief. This discomfort is structural. Refinement removes excess, and excess often feels familiar.

Continuing the work also means accepting asymmetry. The effort you invest in alignment will not always be reciprocated. Others may benefit from your clarity without acknowledging it. Some relationships may only function when you are less congruent. The decision to continue does not depend on validation; it depends on internal consistency.

Compassion remains necessary, but its function changes. It is no longer a justification for delay, nor a shield against responsibility. It becomes a stabilizing force that allows you to act without self-punishment. Compassion sustains effort; it does not replace it.

Patience, too, becomes operational. Not patience with outcomes, but patience with process. Behavioral change rarely proceeds at the pace insight demands. The ability to tolerate incremental progress without abandoning standards determines whether integration holds over time. Continuing the work is not about vigilance at all times. It is about return. You will drift. You will misjudge. You will occasionally act in ways that contradict what you know. What matters is how quickly you notice and how directly you respond. Speed of correction is a more reliable indicator of growth than the absence of error.

This framework does not promise ease. It promises clarity. It does not remove effort; it focuses it. The work continues not because something is missing, but because coherence requires upkeep. There is no final chapter in lived application. Only continued alignment between what you understand and how consistently you choose to act on it.

A Final Reflection

Before moving forward, pause—not to celebrate completion, but to find your bearing. Finishing this book is not an achievement. Remaining willing to confront yourself without distortion is!! That willingness is not a personality trait; it is a practiced stance, and it must be renewed deliberately.

This reflection is not designed to affirm you. It is designed to anchor you. At this stage, acknowledgment must be specific. General pride dissolves under pressure. What endures is clarity about what you now know and what you are therefore responsible for. The purpose of reflection here is to fix reference points before conditions change.

You are about to re-enter environments that will test what you have integrated. Familiar dynamics will resume. Old incentives will reappear. Subtle pressures to abandon coherence in exchange for comfort, approval, or speed will return.

This reflection is meant to function as a stabilizer when those pressures arise. Write a letter to yourself—not as reassurance, but as instruction. Address it from your present self to a future version of you who is tired, distracted, or under strain. Assume that future versions will be tempted to rationalize, to delay, or to compromise quietly. Write accordingly. In this letter, do not describe who you hope to become. Describe what you already understand to be non-negotiable. Name the patterns you can no longer claim ignorance of. Identify the behaviors that erode your self-trust when repeated. Be precise. Include the following elements explicitly:

- **What you now recognize as your most persistent form of self-betrayal**
- **What alignment requires from you when it is least convenient**
- **What cost you are no longer willing to pay for familiarity or ease**
- **What signals indicate that you are drifting and need to recalibrate**

Avoid inspiration. Avoid promises of permanence. Assume fluctuation. This letter is not meant to motivate you in moments of clarity. It is meant to confront you in moments of drift. Its function is recall, not encouragement.

Dear Self,

When you finish writing, do not reread it immediately. Return to it only after you have encountered resistance—after a period where alignment felt effortful, or when avoidance felt justified. The letter should feel corrective, not comforting. This reflection marks a transition in responsibility. Up to this point, insight was being cultivated. From here forward, insight is assumed. What changes is not what you know, but what you tolerate in yourself.

There is no requirement that you be consistent at all times. There is only the requirement that inconsistency be noticed and addressed without delay or self-deception. This is not a closing exercise. It is a reference document. You are not writing to preserve a moment of clarity. You are writing to ensure that clarity survives contact with reality.

Closing Thought

You were never broken.

You were never incomplete.

What was missing was not insight, but ownership of what insight asks of you. Seeing yourself clearly does not dissolve tension; it removes the places where you once hid from it. It does not promise ease. It makes the cost of your choices visible. From here forward, confusion is rarely the obstacle. What remains is willingness.

The mirror is no longer something you turn to for reassurance or explanation. It is simply there to show you, without distortion, where your understanding and your actions align and where they do not. That distance will change. Some days it will narrow. Other days it will widen. What matters is not that it disappears, but that you notice it sooner and respond more honestly. Becoming is not a future version of yourself waiting to arrive. It is shaped quietly, through repetition. Each time you choose alignment over relief, regulation over impulse, and coherence over what feels familiar, you reinforce the direction you are already moving in. There will be moments when pressure dulls your clarity. Old patterns may surface. That does not undo the work; it calls for it. The ability to return, again and again, is not a setback. It is the skill that allows growth to continue when circumstances shift. This book does not ask you to transform yourself. It asks you to stay in a relationship with who you are, consistently, attentively, and with responsibility. It asks you to be consistent.

Not flawless.

Not certain.

But answerable to what you now know.

When you look into the mirror from here on, let it not reflect potential or intention. Let it reflect the pattern. Let it show you, without distortion, whether your actions continue to justify your understanding. The work does not end here. But it no longer needs instruction. Only attention.

Thank you for your vulnerability and taking this journey alongside me!

"Between stimulus and response, there is a space. In that space is our power to choose our response. In our response lies our growth and our freedom."

-Viktor E. Frankl

References

Ahmad, M., Md Din, N. S. B., Tharumalay, R. D., Che Din, N., Ibrahim, N., Amit, N., Farah, N. M., Osman, R. A., Abdul Hamid, M. F., Ibrahim, I. A., Jamsari, E. A., Palil, M. R., & Ahmad, S. (2020). The effects of circadian rhythm disruption on mental health and physiological responses among shift workers and general population. International Journal of Environmental Research and Public Health, 17(19), 7156. https://doi.org/10.3390/ijerph17197156

Alshami, A. M. (2019). Pain: Is it all in the brain or the heart? Current Pain and Headache Reports, 23(12), 88. https://doi.org/10.1007/s11916-019-0827-4

Beck, J. S. (2020). Cognitive behavior therapy: Basics and beyond (3rd ed.). Guilford Press.

Brown, B. (2012). Daring greatly: How the courage to be vulnerable transforms the way we live, love, parent, and lead. Penguin Random House.

Chand, S. P., Kuckel, D. P., & Huecker, M. R. (2026). Cognitive behavior therapy. In StatPearls. StatPearls Publishing. https://www.ncbi.nlm.nih.gov/books/NBK470241/

Clarity Therapy NYC. (n.d.). The stages of trauma and recovery. https://www.claritytherapynyc.com/stages-of-trauma-and-recovery/

Deloitte. (n.d.). World mental health day: A global perspective. https://www.deloitte.com/global/en/issues/work/world-mental-health-day.html

Ekman, P. (n.d.). Universal emotions. https://www.paulekman.com/universal-emotions/

Frankl, V. E. (2006). Man's search for meaning. Beacon Press. (Original work published 1959)

Gainsburg, I., & Kross, E. (2020). Distanced self-talk changes how people conceptualize the self. Journal of Experimental Social Psychology, 88, 103969. https://doi.org/10.1016/j.jesp.2020.103969

Herman, J. L. (1992). Trauma and recovery. Basic Books.

Huberman, A. (n.d.). The science of emotions & relationships. https://www.hubermanlab.com/episode/the-science-of-emotions-relationships

Janowski, K., & Steuden, S. (2020). The temperament risk factor, disease severity, and quality of life in patients with psoriasis. Annals of Dermatology, 32(6), 452–459. https://doi.org/10.5021/ad.2020.32.6.452

Kübler-Ross, E. (1969). On death and dying. Macmillan.

Kyoto2. (n.d.). What are some examples of generational curses? https://www.kyoto2.org/what-are-some-examples-of-generational-curses/

Latinjak, A. T., Morin, A., Brinthaupt, T. M., Hardy, J., Hatzigeorgiadis, A., Kendall, P. C., Neck, C., Oliver, E. J., Puchalska-Wasyl, M. M., Tovares, A. V., & Winsler, A. (2023). Self-talk: An interdisciplinary review and transdisciplinary model. Journal of Personality Assessment.

Ludwig, V., Brown, K. W., & Brewer, J. A. (2020). Self-regulation without force. Perspectives on Psychological Science.

Luo, X., Bartlett, M., & Nicholls, M. E. R. (2025). Stay calm in crowds: Avoiding emotional faces in ensemble perception. Attention, Perception, & Psychophysics, 87(7), 2223–2240. https://doi.org/10.3758/s13414-025-03124-4

Mondal, A., & Gokhale, S. (2020). Mining emotions on Plutchik's wheel. IEEE. https://doi.org/10.1109/SNAMS52053.2020.9336534

Moore, H. (2013). Positive psychology: A path to greater well-being. Global Advances in Health and Medicine, 2(Suppl), S131. https://doi.org/10.7453/gahmj.2013.097CP.P01.02

Moscovitch, D. A., White, K., Hudd, T., et al. (2024). Hooking the self onto the past: How positive autobiographical memory retrieval benefits people with social anxiety. Current Psychology.

Norris, C. J. (2021). The negativity bias, revisited: Evidence from neuroscience measures and an individual differences approach. Social Neuroscience, 16. https://doi.org/10.1080/17470919.2019.1696225

Orvell, A., Vickers, B. D., Drake, B., Verduyn, P., Ayduk, Ö., Moser, J., Jonides, J., & Kross, E. (2021). Does distanced self-talk facilitate emotion regulation across a range of emotionally intense experiences? Social Psychological and Personality Science.

Park, N., & Peterson, C. (2008). Positive psychology and character strengths: Application to strengths-based school counseling. Professional School Counseling, 12(2).

Polyvagal Institute. (n.d.). What is polyvagal theory? https://www.polyvagalinstitute.org/whatispolyvagaltheory

PositivePsychology.com. (n.d.). PERMA model. https://positivepsychology.com/perma-model/

Schwartz, B., Ward, A., Monterosso, J., Lyubomirsky, S., White, K., & Lehman, D. R. (2002). Maximizing versus satisficing: Happiness is a matter of choice. Journal of

Personality and Social Psychology, 83(5), 1178–1197. https://doi.org/10.1037/0022-3514.83.5.1178

Society for Research in Child Development. (2019, December 17). "I will do my very best!" Children who engage in positive self-talk about effort can boost their math achievement. https://www.srcd.org/news/i-will-do-my-very-best-children-who-engage-positive-self-talk-about-effort-can-boost-their

Sternberg, R. J. (1986). A triangular theory of love. Psychological Review, 93(2), 119–135. https://doi.org/10.1037/0033-295X.93.2.119

Szczepańska-Sadowska, E., Wsol, A., Cudnoch-Jedrzejewska, A., & Żera, T. (2021). Complementary role of oxytocin and vasopressin in cardiovascular regulation. International Journal of Molecular Sciences, 22(21), 11465. https://doi.org/10.3390/ijms222111465

Vosgerau, J., et al. (n.d.). Distanced self-talk and emotion regulation benefits. Scientific Reports.

www.ingramcontent.com/pod-product-compliance
Lightning Source LLC
LaVergne TN
LVHW050759061126
851857LV00012B/615
9798256249014